Angel Kids

Angel Kids

Enchanting stories of true-life guardian angels
and 'sixth-sense' abilities in children

Jacky Newcomb

HAY HOUSE

Australia • Canada • Hong Kong
South Africa • United Kingdom • United States

First published and distributed in the United Kingdom by:
Hay House UK Ltd, 292B Kensal Rd, London W10 5BE. Tel.: (44) 20 8962 1230;
Fax: (44) 20 8962 1239. www.hayhouse.co.uk

Published and distributed in the United States of America by:
Hay House, Inc., PO Box 5100, Carlsbad, CA 92018-5100. Tel.: (1) 760 431 7695
or (800) 654 5126; Fax: (1) 760 431 6948 or (800) 650 5115. www.hayhouse.com

Published and distributed in Australia by:
Hay House Australia Ltd, 18/36 Ralph St, Alexandria NSW 2015. Tel.: (61) 2 9669
4299; Fax: (61) 2 9669 4144. www.hayhouse.com.au

Published and distributed in the Republic of South Africa by:
Hay House SA (Pty), Ltd, PO Box 990, Witkoppen 2068. Tel./Fax: (27) 11 467
8904. www.hayhouse.co.za

Published and distributed in India by:
Hay House Publishers India, Muskaan Complex, Plot No.3, B-2, Vasant Kunj, New
Delhi – 110 070. Tel.: (91) 11 4176 1620; Fax: (91) 11 4176 1630.
www.hayhouse.co.in

Distributed in Canada by:
Raincoast, 9050 Shaughnessy St, Vancouver, BC V6P 6E5. Tel.: (1) 604 323 7100;
Fax: (1) 604 323 2600

A catalogue record for this book is available from the British Library.

ISBN 978-1-84850-016-7

Printed and bound by CPI Bookmarque, Croydon CR0 4TD

Ronald Gerald Hill

My darling, much-loved father who became my very own guardian angel during the writing of this book. The greatest fan a girl could ever wish to have ... on Earth, and now in heaven.

I love you, Dad.

Contents

Acknowledgements

I would like to dedicate this book to the members of my Psychic Children Forum, who have been such an inspiration to me. By sharing their personal stories, experiences and suggestions, this book is more useful for readers than it might otherwise have been. Your wisdom as parents of these special children shows how wise these young souls were to choose you as parents in the first place!

Here are a few of their names, with special thanks: Jan Owenby, Sue Taggart, Tracey Bryant, Chance, Cady, Gage Cady, Danielle Bryant, Joshua Cady, Zachary Cady and Brandon Cady. Also Lori Lewis, Christopher Aguiar, Sherri and Coco, Monica Johnson, Lilliana and many more members mentioned throughout the book.

Thank you also to everyone who has written and shared their experiences with me (names added throughout the book where agreed or changed as requested to protect privacy).

❖❖❖❖❖❖

The Psychic Children Forum is a free-to-join Internet group for parents and carers of psychic children (we even have a few psychic children as members themselves).

You can join the group by visiting the following website:

groups.yahoo.com/group/psychic_children/

Extra-special thanks to my own psychic daughters Georgina and Charlotte.

Special thanks to everyone at Hay House, my very supportive literary agent Liz and my PA Debbie Hall (who cleans up the dead mice left by the cats, vacuums around my feet, makes me food, takes care of my mail and organizes my diary ... amongst other things!). Seriously ... thanks!

To Mum, because you believe in me – and, as always, to my dearest husband John.

Introduction

Great spirits have always encountered
opposition from mediocre minds.

Albert Einstein

Magic or Mystic?

All children are extraordinary – but the children included in this book have a little something extra! They live in
a world where 'magic' is real. Where the paranormal is
often an everyday occurrence …

Take Michael, for example. He is one of a growing
number of children who remember his life *before* birth. He
actually recalls choosing his earthly life *before* he was born,
and even picking his Earth-life parents. He *chose* the family
he was going to be born into. Extraordinary, isn't it?

Then there's Angie's daughter. When she was just
three years old it became clear that the young girl had
some extraordinary psychic abilities. The child was able

to pick up information telepathically (mind to mind). She could read her mother's thoughts and even seemed able to know what her mother had been dreaming about the night before!

When asked how she did this, Angie's daughter answered clearly in her own simple language: 'I just *knowed* it in my head!'

Unusual? Not at all. The book is simply filled with such examples.

Is It Real?

Could it really be possible? Indeed it is. Every story in this book is true. Every experience shared by mothers and fathers or relatives and close friends of these psychic children is for real. No one was paid for their stories. No one sought out recognition or fame. Many felt embarrassed or frightened by the experiences. Lots wrote to ask for help or clarification.

Where Are These Children?

Children all over the world are being born with extraordinary psychic abilities These abilities include telekinesis (moving things with the mind), mediumship (the knack of communicating with the deceased) and spiritual healing (using touch or natural objects such as crystals or feathers to help cure illness in those around them). Still others possess the capability of picking up guidance from their guardian angels and spirit guides, unseen by the adults in their lives.

Who Are These Children?

Where do these abilities come from? Maybe we should ask, 'Where do our children come from?' Are our children the souls of advanced spiritual beings who are incarnating on Earth at this time to help our struggling planet, as some believe? Or is this phenomenon part of the natural development of humankind?

Don't think for one minute that this phenomenon is isolated to a small group of 'New Agers'. Stories of children's extraordinary abilities and experiences reach me from all over the world. Some experiences are 'one-offs' which have left the family totally baffled; others are life-long cases where the family just longs to talk to others 'like them' about the fascinating and 'scary' phenomena that they live with on a day-to-day basis.

So What Now?

I've also discovered a few tricks and tips to help develop these abilities and protect the families from some of the more annoying psychic phenomena ... but more about that later!

Parents share their children's secret 'other lives' and also talk about their own psychic childhood experiences. For although it doesn't necessarily follow, there is a trend for psychic parents to produce psychic children. Parents who saw spirits and 'ghosts' as kids seem more likely to produce children who have these abilities ... if not a little stronger than for the previous generation!

Sixth Sense?

I'd also like to explore with you some of the children around the world with sensory abilities outside what we class as *normal*, experiences above and beyond the 'sixth sense'.

During my research I read about children who use their fingertips as their 'eyes' to help them to read or recognize colours. And the extraordinary case of Natasha from Russia, whom they call 'the girl with the X-ray eyes' because of her ability to psychically scan the body for illness and abnormality.

Most of the examples in the book have never been seen in print before. The experiences are shared by ordinary people from around the globe.

I've also taken the time to answer some of the most common questions that parents and guardians ask. My answers are gained from experience with my own kids' psychic phenomena and the many thousands of letters and stories I have studied.

Of course, some of the ideas have come about purely through experimentation (to discover what works and what doesn't). The parents from my online chat group have been most helpful volunteers, and I would like to thank them all for their assistance, and for sharing their stories (many of which are included in this book).

❖❖❖❖❖❖

I've been studying angel and afterlife experiences for many years now, and the number of magical cases involving children has grown and grown. Many families encounter psychic phenomena and 'sixth-sense' abilities from time to time – even if these things happen just once in a lifetime – but for some reason these experiences are happening with greater regularity and to more people than ever … children in particular.

When I was a child I used to watch Samantha the TV witch who would twitch her nose to perform instant magic. But you know what? Nowadays this isn't so far-fetched. I'm not suggesting that a flick of a magic wand will make someone instantly appear or disappear, but some things are just beyond explanation. Some of my youngsters seem to affect electricity and clockwork items, for example, and to have powers that we don't yet understand. Many children appear wise beyond their years.

Passing strangers will peek into a pram and mutter, 'Oh, he looks an old soul …' Perhaps they are right?

I've been fascinated to read about this exciting phenomenon and couldn't wait to share it with you. Won't you join me on a magical journey of discovery?

While we try to teach our children all about life,
Our children teach us what life is all about.

Angela Schwindt

CHAPTER I

Angel Kids

There are more things in heaven and earth, Horatio, than
are dreamt of in your philosophy.

William Shakespeare, Hamlet I.v.166–7

A World of Make-believe?

Children are really amazing, aren't they? They already
live in a world of magic and enchantment. They create life and games from the simplest of things. Whole
worlds emerge out of cardboard boxes. Simple petticoats
and sparkly necklaces become costumes for princes and
princesses, and silver foil becomes crowns and swords
for kings and knights. Teddies and dolls emerge as special friends and important cast members. One wave of a
tinsel wand and the magic begins.

But what of the childhood 'imaginary' friends that
many children play with? Are these invisible compan-
ions always 'made up', or is it possible that, on occasion,
our children's 'make-believe' characters are real?

What Is Real?

Open your mind for just one moment. Is it possible that things exist even though we can't see them? Is it likely that something might be there even though we can't hear it? Is it feasible that something exists even though we are unable to feel or touch it? Of course it's possible ... and probable, according to the laws of physics!

We already have things in our world which we can't perceive with our limited human senses. We use radio waves to send and receive messages ... but we can't see them; we just know they exist because the radio works when we turn it on. This is just the tip of the iceberg. There are colours and sounds (vibrations) that human senses cannot perceive but science shows us are there.

Bugs and germs can make us ill (and even kill us) but are completely invisible to the human eye ... yet no one would argue that they don't exist.

Some scientists now agree that there is new evidence that existence is multi-dimensional in nature. This reality is one that has already been believed by Hindus, Buddhists and Kabbalists for thousands of years.

Our world, as we know it, exists in four dimensions (time, height, width and length) but it is likely to exist in more than 11 dimensions according to many experts. What we see, hear and feel isn't all there is ... Of course it's very likely that there are many more than 11 dimensions, and quite possibly thousands of them. Our limited human minds might never get our heads around that conundrum!

What Is 'Normal'?

Is it probable, then, that some children, young children in particular, are able to perceive more than what we perceive as *normal*? There have always been people who are 'psychic' and have the ability to pick up more than the 'average' (remember we used to burn 'witches' in England – which wasn't very nice!). It's typical of the human race to harm something of which it is afraid.

It seems likely that the human race is developing at such a rate that many children born today are able to tune into and see, hear and experience some of these other realms of existence that have been unavailable to humankind up until this point. (Or at least unavailable to most of us).

Does It Exist Even When We Cannot See It?

Many years ago I remember feeding my baby daughter late into the night when she suddenly pulled away from her milk and focused on something to the side of us. The room was dark and I was only able to see her face lit up by the light coming from the open bathroom door, yet my daughter was mesmerized by something totally unseen to me. My small baby daughter began to giggle. Something was highly amusing. I wish I could have shared the joke with her. What did she see? Who was there?

Other mums report this strange phenomenon. It happened with both my children and on several occasions. Can our children see their guardian angels, their spiritual guides, deceased relatives or something else? Maybe on occasion it is all of these and more. Here is Melanie's story.

Daughter Sees Spirits

My daughter Emily is eight years old and she has been very lonely at school since her best friend moved to Australia! Yesterday she said to me, 'Do you believe in ghosts?' I told her I did, and she explained that she had a ghost friend named George. Emily explained that George was five but would be six the following day. She told me that she had played with him in the playground at school and that it was only when the whistle blew at the end of playtime and George disappeared into the light that she'd realized he wasn't a real boy.

George also appears at night-time and tells Emily not to be afraid of him because he just wants to be her friend. She described him in great detail, including that he has no hair. George explained that he had lost his hair when he was alive because he was ill, but that now he was feeling better and so his hair was starting to grow back.

Emily explained that George always wears a blue jacket and grey shorts or trousers ... except when it's Emily's bathtime. Then George changes into a blue swimsuit with arms!

I asked Emily how long she has been friends with George and she said ages, but that George had asked her to tell her mother now because it was his birthday the following day.

Melanie bought George a birthday cake so that they could celebrate the birthday of the little ghost boy! Melanie also tells me that, although Emily is a normal little girl and, at eight, is starting to be a little cheeky, George tells her to be a good girl for her mummy and that it's her own fault if she gets told off! It hardly sounds like the sort of thing a child might make up.

Emily explained that George only whispers to her and that no one else can see him. When other people are in the room he appears as a small light, but if she is on her own or with her baby sister he is a real boy and wants to play. George goes to school with her but only plays in the playground; if she is in class he is just a light. It sounds like George has morals!

Melanie explains,

It seems such a lot of information for an eight-year-old to imagine. Emily has seen things before as well. My granddad Bob died 12 years ago, so Emily never saw him, but when she was three she started talking to her friend 'Bob'. One day we went to visit my mum to go through some old family photographs; as soon as Emily saw one of my granddad she asked, 'Why do you have a photograph of my friend Bob?'

How do you answer that one? I guess it's possible that Emily had seen a photograph of Bob before. Maybe her grandmother had brought out the family photographs in the past. Or maybe not!

Debbie's story is adorable.

Oh Yes, You Are …

My son Ellis is very special to me, as are all my children, but he seems to have a gift that I think is so special. He has been photographed by my parents playing with his cousins in their garden, and in two separate photographs you can see a foggy whiteness just to the side and around him. I always used to think that was his spirit guide or guardian angel.

Several unusual things have happened over the years but one memorable incident was when he was eight years old. I was sitting on my bed relaxing and reading a book when Ellis came into my bedroom.

He climbed up on my bed and said to me, 'Mummy, my baby brother's growing in your tummy.'

I was 'gobsmacked' to say the least. 'No, he's not, Ellis,' I said. 'You see, Mummy isn't having any more babies; I have you and Nina.'

Ellis looked at me, smiling, and said, undeterred, 'Mummy, I think you'll find that he is, and in just over six months I'll be able to play with him!'

I uttered a few more dismissive words to him and sent him on his way. I smiled to myself about the whole incident but I was not due a period for another three days, and anyhow I had not planned another baby. We were in the middle of a house-build and I was 39 years old!

Three days came and went and my period did not arrive, so I took a trip to the local supermarket and purchased a pregnancy test. I was astonished when the test showed that I was pregnant! Needless to say, I was not thrilled about it at first!

Four months later I had my scan and I said to the woman doing the scan, 'It's a boy, isn't it?' after telling her my story. She confirmed that it was. When I told Ellis he just smiled and said, 'See, I told you so, Mum.'

I sat Ellis down one day and asked how he knew his brother was coming. He told me that he had longed for a baby brother and on this particular day he heard someone tell him that his brother was going to be born. Perhaps it was even new baby Callum himself?

Ellis and his sister Nina have adored Callum from the moment they laid eyes on him. They have a wonderful relationship with their baby brother. I guess he really was meant to be here with us after all.

Visitors from Other Realms and Dimensions?

Later in the book I will explore some of the reasons behind these new experiences found in children today. Is it possible that we are being assisted in our human growth by those who exist in other dimensions, or even races? It's certainly a theory worth investigating, as I have been stunned by the amazing stories of children interacting with, visiting and being visited by extraterrestrial visitors.

For years, people who profess to alien encounters have been ridiculed by the public. Yet is it probable that an innocent child would make up such a story? I think it unlikely.

Author Mike Oram is one of the people who have generously shared their experiences. We'll read a lot more about Mike's fascinating lifelong encounters later in the book. It certainly gives you 'food for thought', and I promise that you'll be stunned by these sincere accounts.

Visitor from the Other Side of Life?

I am most intrigued by the stories of children who see deceased relatives. Parents, grandparents and siblings seem to be the most common visitors, with children often receiving visits from loved ones that they have never even met in life … just like Emily's visits from her great-granddad Bob!

Death shows no boundaries for love. I think it's wonderful to know that our little ones are being looked after and protected by their own 'guardian angels' from another side of life.

Pets as Co-psychics and Visitors

Our youngsters are as confused by the phenomena they experience as are the adults around them. Pets feature in many of the experiences that have been shared with me. Jan shared this next real-life story.

Dog Validation?

At four years old my grandson asked me about the man he could see through. He wanted to know why he could see through him (good question). He's eight now, and in the last few years he has seen many different 'spirits' (he doesn't use the word 'ghost'). I try my best not to push ideas into his head, and think it's important to just let him talk when he wants to and ask questions if he needs to. He has problems with sleeping (he sees orb-like lights at night), although he's fine as long as someone lies down with him. We believe the land we live on has a lot of Native American history attached to it. So far Alex has seen two different Native Americans (both on horseback). The first time Alex saw a Native American, our dog was upset and staring out of the French doors. We looked out and I didn't see anything, but then Alex came by and said, 'Oh, he sees the man on the horse.'

Many of my readers believe that their pets are psychic. I believe that they can see and hear on a different 'vibrational' level from us. We just know that the silent dog whistles are only silent to humans! What's great about Jan's story is that the dog appears to validate her grandson's experience! Useful for the sceptic!

So many of the children mentioned in the book have abilities which are quite unexplainable. There are so many different types of ability, and I want to explore them all with you.

Jennifer told me about her extraordinary daughter, Lilli.

How Did She Know?

My older son was sent home sick from school. My daughter Lilli goes to pre-school, *after* her brother gets on the bus. Lilli had seen her brother get on the bus that morning, but when I went to pick her up from school that afternoon, she asked me, 'Mommy, why is Anthony at home already?' How did she know? I know for certain that I had not mentioned his coming home to her!

Then, a couple of days ago, I was looking at some pictures on my sister's website (she is a photographer, and also freelances in photo-editing). I was looking at a photo she had edited of a baby girl named Harley (like the name of the motorbike). Lilli cannot read yet, but she walked into the room as I was scrolling down to read some comments on the picture, and she said, 'Mommyyyyyyyy … go back to the motorcycle girl!'

Ready for the Evidence?

So what are we dealing with here? Coincidence? Confusion? Forgetfulness? Misunderstandings? Are parents reading more into their experiences than is really there?

What at first seems a long stretch for the mind becomes more and more believable and understandable as the readers' true tales begin to stack up.

None of these cases is an isolated incident. Remember, this research has taken me years to assemble.

Are you ready to start exploring some paranormal abilities? We're only just getting warmed up!

CHAPTER 2

Psychic Abilities: Sixth Sense and Beyond

The most beautiful thing we can experience is the
mysterious. It is the source of all true art and all
science. He to whom this emotion is a stranger, who
can no longer pause to wonder and stand rapt in
awe, is as good as dead: his eyes are closed.

Albert Einstein

Many adults experience sixth-sense abilities … those
abilities which seem to fall outside the 'normal' param-
eters. We expect to be able to use our five regular senses
(sight, sound, touch, taste and smell). But as humans we
have the ability for so much more!

Just because we do not understand these things, it
doesn't mean that they don't exist … ask any mother! As
my own mum used to say, '… I need eyes in the back
of my head' (to be able to look after her three young
daughters!). I am sure she DID have eyes in the back of

her head, because she always knew what we were up to! I'm sure, too, that like most parents of young children we rely on our intuition as much as any other ability when it comes to protecting our young.

In children these unexplainable abilities seem all the more dramatic because of the innocence of a child. You know that a youngster is not trying to trick you or lie to you, and the younger the child the more sixth-sense abilities there seem to be. To the child, however, these abilities are normal.

How Can These Things Exist?

So many thousands of children, worldwide, can see, hear and feel things which most adults cannot. Yet we know for sure that everything we see isn't everything there is. Science already knows this for sure. The visible light spectrum (that small bit that our human eyes can perceive) is such a teeny bit of what exists, for example.

Our human bodies are ill-equipped to pick up anything but the smallest possibility of what might ... and does ... exist. I've said it in my books before and I will say it again – even dogs and cats can see and hear more than we can! It's stupid and naïve to believe that everything we can see, hear and feel is everything there is! Of course it isn't!

Imagine, then, that many children of recent years have expanded abilities and opened up their consciousness just a little bit more than we are used to. I don't profess to have all the answers, or even most of them, but I do have some suggestions for some of the phenomena I am about to share with you in this book.

The stories in this chapter cover a very wide range of phenomena. Some things will intrigue you and yet others might frighten you. Others will fascinate you – but many will confuse your mind, as they do mine. Humans are often frightened of what they don't understand – it's a natural defence mechanism.

Is It Logical?

Many children have experienced things in their lives that seem impossible to our logical minds. If you have no personal experience of psychic phenomena your mind will find it even more of a struggle, yet I promise you these things are really happening.

I'm not asking you to read every chapter. In fact, I suggest that if certain chapters frighten you, leave them and come back to them another time. Allow your mind to expand just a little bit at a time. If you don't feel ready to face certain phenomena, then leave them for now. Read when you are ready. You might breeze through the book in one go (especially if you have read my work in the past), but if this is new to you it may give you more than a little food for thought. Take your time.

You might prefer to read a chapter and put the book down. Go about your business, do normal things and read something which is not related to the paranormal. When you have digested the material in that chapter, choose another, and then another. On the other hand, you might be like many of my readers who can't put the book down between chapters.

As you read through the book you may experience some of the following thoughts about the material:

- I always knew about this stuff.
- This writer is crazy!
- Can this be real?
- This is a load of rubbish!
- This is what has been happening to me.
- Of course … that explains everything!
- This is fascinating!
- I can't wait to learn more …
- I don't understand it, so it can't be real.

I want you to remember those other sayings of the past:

- The Earth is flat.
- It's impossible for man to fly.
- Of course humankind can't visit the moon.

Remember, too, the difficulties that many people have with sharing this sort of information. Lindsay told me how hard it was not to be believed as a child.

He Really Came!

When I was 16 my granddad passed away, and the week after that he started playing games! One day when I went with my mum into her office, he knocked all the papers off a desk, and on another day we felt him around and he created cold spots on a very hot June day in an office with no air-conditioning and no fan. Within a week of the funeral I had my GCSE exams. Granddad came to me in my sleep, my first dream visitation. I told people I wasn't dreaming; I know I wasn't dreaming. This was a real visit. But I was met with ridicule and told that, although they understood that I *wished* it were true, it wasn't!

During the visit he sat on my bed and I felt the pressure on the bedclothes as he sat down. I hid my head under my duvet and he laughed. He said it would all be OK, without actually talking with his mouth. I just heard him, not as though he was talking normally, but in my head, like a thought, but not *my* thoughts.

In later years my nan told me that she believed me, and she wished she'd seen him herself. Apparently her own mother came to visit her in a dream on a few occasions. I really wished she'd told me about her own experiences at the time. Then everything would've made perfect sense!

How Do You Know If You *Were* or *Have* a Psychic Child?

If you have a child in your family who is already exhibiting expanded awareness, or if you yourself have witnessed or experienced psychic phenomena as a child, then you are already one step ahead.

Some people have begun to classify different types of psychic children depending on when they were born and other distinguishing factors such as behaviour or appearance.

You might hear names such as 'Indigo Child' (children exhibiting a lot of the colour indigo in their aura or energy field, the so-called 'first wave' of new children), 'Crystal Children', 'Rainbows' (whom some believe to be the most recent wave) or more general terms such as 'Children of the New World', 'Sky Children' and 'Star Children'.

Let's look at some of the behaviour patterns and phenomena based around these new psychic children. Do you recognize any of these?

- difficulty fitting into the traditional school system
- spend a lot of time on their own
- have 'invisible' friends
- have a close affinity to animals or a deep connection which seems to go beyond 'normal'
- animals are attracted to them and often seem unafraid

- very attracted to crystals, water and other natural objects
- become extraordinarily upset if animals, birds or even insects become hurt or die
- react in a strong negative way if plants and trees are damaged
- to others may seem to express behavioural difficulties
- suffer with allergies
- get bored easily
- have been diagnosed with attention deficit disorder or similar, autism or Asperger's syndrome (amongst others)
- are happier out in nature
- are nurturing, loving and giving
- sometimes show healing abilities
- are often slow to start speaking because they rely on their natural telepathic abilities to pick up and send information non-verbally
- are drawn to help others (especially other children) who are sick, frightened or in danger
- want to change the world for the better and become disturbed at the way the public in general misuse the Earth
- have a keen interest in ecological and green issues
- see things or hear things that others do not
- photographs often reveal that the children are surrounded by or next to balls (orbs) or flashes of light (not visible to the naked eye)

- appear interested and knowledgeable about world issues at a young age
- have strong personalities yet at the same time may appear very laid-back
- are very creative
- are empathic
- are spiritual
- paranormal, unexplainable and unusual things happen around them
- are sensitive both physically and emotionally, often picking up on the emotions of others around them
- sometimes talk about living somewhere else before they came here
- talk about their 'other home' or 'other parents'
- sometimes feel they don't belong here
- their social behaviour appears 'different' from the norm, or they have problems fitting in with normal social interaction
- balk at authority
- are blunt and truthful
- often possess large or very expressive eyes
- suffer sleep problems, nightmares or disrupted sleep
- seem to tune in on your thoughts and feelings easily
- affect / interfere with or manipulate electrical objects around them
- talk about strange concepts
- occasionally use difficult and complicated language beyond their age
- often hand out advice to adults in a way that seems way beyond their years … and is right!

Little Healers

I used to have a little meditation room at my old house. Like many children, my young daughter was fascinated by my crystal collection, which was spread around the room.

One day I was lying on the floor with a raging headache. 'Can I help, Mummy?' my little girl asked kindly. I wondered how she might be able to assist me, but she pointed to the crystals in a knowing way. 'Sure,' I replied.

Well, Georgina proceeded to select a handful of crystals and place them all over my body as I lay on the floor. I had no idea why or how she might have got the idea, but it was keeping her quiet! I had no expectations.

I kept my eyes firmly closed, and relaxed. Minutes later she lifted the crystals off me and proceeded to wave a feather over my body. What was she doing? She seemed confident in her abilities to heal my headache … and do you know what? My headache had gone. Was it just a coincidence or had Georgina healed my headache using the ancient art of crystal healing?

I praised her skills and asked her where she had learned her technique. 'I don't know but I just know,' she said confidently. I have no clue how my little girl learned crystal healing. Is it an ability that she 'brought with her' at birth? Is she an 'old soul' who has always known these things, or had she caught the tail end of a TV programme when I had been out of the room?

I later did some research and discovered that lots of healers 'smooth down the aura' (the body's natural energy field) using a feather after a healing experience, just as she had done instinctively. Strange …!

Monica's daughter is a healer – and it seems like it might be hereditary!

Little Healing Hands

I have three children aged between eight and 14. I have received visions my entire life (along with severe migraines), and only in the past five or six years have I finally realized that I had been trying to 'block' my visions my whole life. My mother always told me it was 'crazy talk'. Once I started owning and believing in myself and my feelings (and moving away from the area where my mother lived!) I finally stopped having the constant migraines.

My daughter Samantha has been talking to spirits since she was two years old, and I didn't want to be like my mother and put her off what was a natural ability for her. I wanted to give her accurate information and advice so that she could strengthen her gifts from God.

As she got older we also started realizing that she could heal animals. She can heal people, too, but I haven't encouraged that as much. I have severe health problems myself along with constant pain, and have to wear a pain patch all the time. I have only asked my daughter for help on two occasions. Both times the pain was so severe (and it was the middle of the night) that I actually had my husband wake her up. As she laid her hands on me I felt warmth coming from her hands and could feel the pain being literally pulled out of me. In less than ten minutes she had removed the pain completely.

Now, the reason I haven't asked her to heal me of everything else is because I honestly don't know what her powers do to *her* body. (She has shown symptoms of many of my problems since she was young.) I'm afraid that she will either absorb my problems and have to suffer like I do, or not be able to completely heal me and then lose faith in her abilities.

If I should get worse or even die, I don't want her to think she really doesn't have a gift because she couldn't completely heal me.

Although it's unlikely that Samantha would be personally harmed by using her healing abilities, it's useful for her to learn how to 'channel' her healing energy safely. Imagine when that annoying friend rings you at all hours of the day and night and chats and moans for hours and hours. All the while you are being sympathetic and listening to your friend, but at the end of the phone call your friend says, 'Thank you, I feel loads better …' but YOU are now exhausted!

Although you might not be aware of it, your friend on the phone is a psychic 'vampire' – not literally a vampire, of course, but taking and draining you of your energy! Neither of you is aware at the time that this is happening, but the effects are clear afterwards.

So, if you have a young healer in the family, teach them to let the healing energy pass through them … rather than giving away their own energy. (See Chapter 9 for more details of how to do this.)

Telepathy

Many parents have experience of this. I remember wondering about things absent-mindedly and then discovering that my child was responding to my unasked questions! Very small children can often do this, but then lose the ability as they get older and learn to speak and respond using more traditional methods!

Many of us have one-off occasions when we have picked up a word, phrase or thought from a close loved one. Our minds are often daydreaming at the same time. I regularly do this with my husband, as he does with me. It's like we are able to listen in on each other's musings – momentarily, that is. We sort of 'tune into' each other's thought frequency in the way we might tune into a radio station. I'm sure that scientists in years to come will understand how – and why – we do this!

In psychic children this ability goes above and beyond this occasional and spontaneous phenomenon. They can even pick up our personal and private thoughts unless we learn to hide them away!

Angie, whom I mentioned in the Introduction, is well aware of her own daughter's psychic and healing abilities. She has the added ability of using mind-to-mind communication (telepathy) and telekinesis (moving objects with her mind).

Mind Reader

My daughter is now eight years old and she is a healer. This all started about four years back, and although we understand it a little bit more now, it was very surprising at first.

Only our family and a few friends know about what my daughter can do. I kind of knew she was a bit psychic when she was around two or three, because she saw a spirit one morning and told me about it. I knew it was true just by her demeanour.

I never in my wildest dreams ever thought she would be a healer, though. She has also been able to tell me what I have dreamt about the night before. She can also move a crayon or pencil in her hand just by using her energy.

She sometimes knows things, and when I ask her how she knows, her reply is always, 'I just *knowed* it in my head!'

Telekinesis – Moving Objects with the Power of the Mind

Angie's daughter shows early natural ability to move things by the power of her thoughts. Older children seem to develop this skill, and as they reach adulthood their abilities are ready to put to practical use (to help others, which is why I believe they have the gifts in the first place).

This ability can also manifest in other ways. Some people can't wear a watch, for example, because their watches always break or keep the wrong time. Some believe this is because the aura or energy field of the advanced psychic person interferes with the quartz crystal which helps the watch keep the correct time ... but this ability can also charge batteries, too. Not every psychic person affects energy in this way, however (I don't, for example).

Others find that light bulbs blow and computers go haywire when they're nearby. Some youngsters seem to be able to manipulate remote controls, switch things off and on using their minds, and move simple objects like pins or paper using their minds.

You'll forgive me if we don't always use individuals' real names in these stories. Naturally parents, although willing to share their stories to help others, are not keen on having their children scientifically tested!

Here is another example, then. Let's call this young woman 'Sally'.

Daunting Abilities

I am 18 and I have always had strange abilities, but at the moment I can't control them. They pop up at some of the worst times, too! I have also read up on PK abilities (psycho-kinesis, a type of mind over matter which is a skill used to bend and move things) because whenever I get highly emotionally distressed, power outages happen around me. When this happens, everything in my mind goes black and it feels like I am not even here. Then when I come out of it, either the lights have blown out or the lights are flickering. I got extremely emotionally distraught on one occasion and I blacked out. When I came out of it, my whole town had lost power! It was on the news that something had happened to a generator!

Could the temper of a young girl have the ability to shut down the power of a whole town? It's an interesting thought! Sally continues,

Lately I have discovered more of a defensive ability. Over Halloween I was visiting my friend's mom and her son Craig. While they were eating outside, they asked me if I wanted to eat something. I didn't, but Craig – who is only a toddler – walked up to me and gave me some corn and told me to eat. (I was very emotional and upset at this point because there were a lot of rumours going around about me.) Because Craig asked me to, I took the corn kindly and held it in my hand.

Well, then I decided to have a good old-fashioned food fight, so I flicked the piece of corn (gently) towards him. He smiled, then scooped up a chicken leg, mashed potato and corn and went to throw the whole lot at me (his mother was eating and reading an article, so she wasn't paying attention). I thought I had better act quickly – especially as it was my fault. So, right as he pulled his arm back, instinct kicked in and I closed my eyes and yelled, 'NO!' very loudly. When I opened my eyes (and it was odd, as it didn't feel like anything was real) I saw little Craig fly backwards, slide five feet across the porch and almost fall! He looked at me with shock and horror. We both knew something strange had happened. Now, Craig can also see spirits and he communicates with them, so I think he realized the connection! I felt horrible about it, and of course I would never want to hurt anyone.

The very next day my friend and I were walking downtown trying to get across some heavy traffic and no one would stop. One car came flying down the road going about 60 miles an hour. I instinctively shut my eyes and screamed in my head, 'Just STOP!'

Well, I opened them right as the van was in front of the crosswalk, and saw that the van had stopped very suddenly. The driver hadn't hit the breaks, either. It looked like the van had hit some invisible force – the back end had lifted up about a foot as well. I don't know who was more surprised, me or the van driver. He seemed to be freaking out and had no idea what had just happened to him.

Are these things connected? Was Sally actually manipulating the energy around her?

Learning any new skill takes time and practice. But intent is everything. Sally is just learning to recognize her abilities, but in the long term her natural-born skill must be used with care. God-given gifts like this one are not for personal gain and not to be used to manipulate the free will of others … but she is very wise and knows this already!

I know in my heart that Sally's stories are genuine. I also believe that she has psychic abilities at work here. I also know that she will learn to use these abilities wisely.

One woman told me,

I have a mint-condition Care Bear watch from the early eighties. It's in perfect condition but the only thing is that after 25 years or so the battery, of course, is dead. I put it on and naturally it didn't work; I knew it wouldn't. The seller even told me that the battery was dead, as would be expected. Then my daughter put the watch on and it worked. So I know there is something unusual about her energy; I'm just not exactly sure what!

A few years ago I had reprimanded her for something, and she was as mad as a hornet. She was probably close to being five at the time. She was fuming and folded her arms and just glared at me in rage. The closest electrical thing to her was the garage door (I usually keep it closed as a safety feature to keep wild animals out), but on this occasion the garage door was open. During her rage we saw the door close all on its own, and neither of us had pushed the button. Garage doors don't automatically shut themselves, and I knew immediately it was because of my daughter's effect on the electricity!

Precognition

Precognition is *knowing* what's about to happen before it happens. This is a difficult skill to track because the ability often shows itself in picture form. These images have to be interpreted by the human brain, and this is where things can go awry. Visions of future events often occur during dream states. I suggest that any such visions are recorded either on computer or in a notebook (or ask your child to do the same, or record them for your child if the child cannot write). The notepad option can be easier because you can keep a notepad and pen by the bed. Write down your vision with as much information as you can remember. Date your entries.

Sally, mentioned earlier in this chapter, also has premonitions. She told me,

> ... psychic ability does run in my family, and my mother told me my brother used to have premonitions and visions. I used to have visions and premonitions a lot, too, and now they have developed into me just knowing what's going to happen without the horrible dreams.

Many children have combinations and variations of these abilities. Sheryl told me,

Mind Reading and Beyond

From time to time my daughter Kara uses mind-reading abilities. She will also sometimes blurt out something very personal from my distant past, from when I was a little girl myself (even if I am not thinking about it at the time).

I don't know how you classify these abilities: knowing things from others' pasts; knowing birth dates and ages of other people; saying something, then having it happen.

She even knows if something will work or not before we try it out. There was one occasion when we were all at the park. I was going to drink some water at the water fountain, but Kara casually said, 'It's not working,' and it wasn't. But it had been working the last time we'd visited the park, so how did she know?

When she was four, I had a weird experience. I was asleep on the couch because I wasn't feeling well. Kara was asleep in her bed. Then I woke up and I could see Kara standing in front of the television, just looking at me. I called out her name and she just evaporated in front of my eyes. I was very freaked out! I ran into her bedroom and found her sound asleep in bed!

One night my husband Jody was sleeping on the couch. Like many men, he regularly falls asleep in front of the television. Kara came into the living room and snuggled up to him on the couch and went to sleep too. Jody said he was having a dream where he was taking a short-cut to someplace. When he woke up from his dream, Kara was looking at him. She asked him, 'Daddy, why are you taking a short-cut?' It was as if she had been sharing the same dream, and I've never heard Jody talk in his sleep before so it's not as if that could be an explanation.

Since Kara could speak she has read minds, and at times this can be very unsettling. Over time, though, I have learned to block it a little – but she can still pick up information from others without any trouble. For example, she will know what's going on at my friend's house even though it's 40 miles away. Physical distance is no problem. Kara will make me call my friend to ask why she is yelling at her daughter!

My friend's daughter is also psychic. She is very intelligent and has an IQ of 165. It's very unnerving when a seven-year-old corrects all of your mistakes! Anyway, both girls can – and do – do extraordinary things.

Monica wrote to tell me about her daughter Sammi, who has several different types of abilities including telepathy. 'My daughter answered my husband a couple of times before he'd actually asked her a question. So now she is reading our minds, too!'

Psychic children often have other children around them with similar abilities. This might be a sibling, cousin or just a school friend.

Some might believe that this sort of precognition can be frightening, but in most cases the families find the information comforting. This story from a woman called Kathryn is an extreme case, but seems to prove the point. I'll let her explain.

We're So Sorry ...

My second daughter (when she was a pre-schooler) told us the actual day of the week that my mother-in-law would pass away, so we know that she is sensitive.

My youngest daughter came to me two days before my husband John was due to undergo supposedly simple surgery and said that her grandmother (who'd passed away when my youngest was just a year old) had visited her. She described her as a younger woman, as I had never seen her, but my husband recognized the description right away.

She said her grandmother told her that 'We are sorry, we don't know what went wrong with the surgery,' and 'We are waiting for John.' Knowing her psychic abilities, this alarmed us, and we prepared as best we could. Both girls were very anxious about his surgery and didn't like the 'darkness growing' in and around Daddy. John's simple benign tumour was diagnosed as Stage 4 terminal cancer, which had spread to his lungs, liver and more. They (his daughters) knew he was dying before the doctors did. Six months, the doctors say. Less, according to our daughters, but we don't press them.

Laughter is the best medicine, so I will leave you with this. One thing my daughters warned me about was that 'Daddy will be angry about his vitals.' This made no sense at the time, but while in hospital I let my husband know, 'Honey, I took your watch, your ring and your wallet. I have them.' Still in a morphine fog, he answered, 'OK, but the nurse just took my vitals [vital signs, blood pressure, pulse] and I want them back. I might need them!'

He will leave us laughing to the very end.

Mediumship

Mediumship is such a common ability among psychic children that I have devoted a large part of this book to the subject.

Let's look a little at how this ability might come about. The new psychic children have enhanced senses. They can pick up more than has previously been classed 'normal' to the human body. Now, whether this is natural evolution or you believe (or wish to explore) some of the other possibilities in the book as to how this ability comes about … is up to you. But to ignore it is no longer a possibility. Many, many thousands of children *are* being born with these extra abilities, and mediumship is one of them. Believe it or not, it's up to you … but it's happening anyway!

Many consider that the spirit realms (heaven) and spirits (mainly the souls of our deceased loved ones), are right here beside us. Their realm literally overlaps our own. Most of us can't perceive this realm – with our limited human abilities. Our eyes cannot see what is right here with us, our ears cannot hear even as well as our domestic pets. But it's not our fault! The human body is ill-equipped to cope with these higher vibrational ranges.

Near Death

When people have the classic 'near-death experience', following the physical death of the human body, they find themselves being pulled down a tunnel with a bright light at the end. Now, most people (assuming they are not going to die at this point) are sent back to their bodies – they literally are told, 'Turn back, it's not your time,' by deceased relatives they see in this tunnel, or others they believe to be their guardian angels.

On rare occasions people go through the light at the end of the tunnel and get a glimpse of heaven on the other side. Some people see colours that are not of this Earth – beautiful colours that they cannot describe because there is no reference from which to do this. There are many more colours (and sights and sounds) than our limited human bodies can perceive; our souls are able to experience so much more.

The new breed of psychic children seems to be able to access these higher-level abilities either because their bodies are more highly developed or because they are able (through their own 'natural' psychic ability), to pick up more than the 'normal' human being has been capable of. Seeing spirits is one of these abilities.

Most children are very happy about their ability. To them, it is commonplace. The difficulties arise when those around them are unable to see, feel and hear these spirits for themselves. The fear or even annoyance of others can (temporarily) shut down these children's abilities. Any adult psychic who, when still a child, shut down their own natural abilities will tell you that it happened because they were not believed or *told off* about it.

Tamy's daughter learned to cope with her visions as long as she could, and then spoke about them when she felt ready. Tamy tells us,

I See Dead People

My daughter has just turned 12 and I always suspected that she could see spirits. Up until this point she had totally denied being able to see or do anything unusual, except for one time when she did admit to seeing a little girl in our hallway crying for her mother.

Well, I'm not sure what happened but we were talking yesterday and she's finally admitted that she has always seen, heard and communicated with spirits her whole life, even when we are out in public. She told me yesterday (after I had mentioned that our house has seemed so empty lately).

We had a fire in the kitchen in February and

remodelled the entire thing. My daughter told me that the spirits weren't very happy about it at all, and constantly showed this by hiding tools and even dumping a deep-fat fryer all over the floor. She told me that they were extremely angry about us redoing the kitchen and that they'd left the house.

I took the opportunity to ask about the little girl crying for her mother, because I hadn't seen or felt her for quite a while, either. It was such a beautiful thing because my daughter told me that the little girl's mother finally came to get her! She said she woke up one night around midnight and felt someone in her room, and the little girl told her goodbye! I am just so excited for her! I guess I'm also excited for me, because this is such a huge breakthrough for my little girl to finally trust me enough to share with me what has been going on in her life.

My son is psychic too, but won't talk about it. He said he was told he wasn't allowed to tell anyone about whatever he's seeing at the moment.

Many children who work on these higher realms feel they have a mission to accomplish – it's not that they are trying to keep things from us so much as they (and their spirit teachers) feel we (us mere mortals!) won't understand or be ready for the information they have to impart. It's kind of mind-blowing, isn't it?

Unless your child is being harmed mentally or you have difficulties with normal behaviour, then maybe it's best to just let things pan out. Of course, if you are lucky enough that your child feels they can talk to you about their experiences, then so much the better.

Each child will usually choose someone to tell – but be prepared for the fact that this might not be you. Be prepared for them to talk to your partner, a grandparent, family friend or teacher (in many cases the child will confide in a sibling or close friend).

It's worth bearing in mind, too, that secrets can be dangerous. Do take care that any 'secrets' your child refers to are, indeed, psychic ones. At all times, the utmost care of the child must, of course, take priority.

If your child is receiving contact from the spirit of family members and friends who have passed over, this can have advantages to other members of the (living) family. Your child might have a loving message for you. If you listen carefully to spontaneous messages, you might discover that 'Grandma has arrived safely on the other side of life' or that 'Granddad suggests you check the brakes on your car!'

Christa's daughter was getting regular visits from spirits and this was causing problems with her sleeping at night. Grandpa now acts as a gatekeeper, or a sort of bouncer or guardian to keep away unwanted spirits during the night. She told me,

Guardian Grandad

My 14-year-old daughter Alexandra finds that spirits are increasingly attracted to her (spirits know that she can see them, and they all have important messages to pass on to someone on the earthly plane!). Of course, this can be very annoying!

Right now spirits are regularly visiting her, although she is unable to converse with them. Alexandra has told me that my maternal grandfather has stopped unwanted ones from coming into the house when she is sleeping. Since he has made his presence known, only one strange spirit has awoken her from her sleep. This spirit was lovingly caressing her head when she woke up. She knew this was not her Grandpa and came running down the stairs to tell me.

I have a feeling it was someone from our family, because Alexandra did not want to hurt its feelings by telling it to go away. It is just a lot less spooky for us when we can know who it is.

A couple of weeks ago Alex had a bad cold. I gave her some cold medicine to help her sleep. She fell into a deep sleep and a little girl came to her in her dream. She was about eight or nine, in a hospital gown, bald head (Alex thinks she was a cancer victim). She was trying to tell Alex something, but Alex was not able to hear what she was saying. Alex said there was blackness all around the child. Far behind this little girl was a brilliant white light.

I find it interesting that Alex saw the 'blackness' around the children with cancer in the same way that Kathryn's children saw the blackness around their dying father.

Some abilities take time to develop. In this example the little girl is able to make contact with some family members, but finds it harder with unknown spirits. Child spirits are especially attracted to living human children, especially when there are toys in the bedroom – more of this later!

Although we can perceive these visits as scary or spooky, when we look at them logically they are not. Most children are only scared if we are!

A woman called Zea told me the following story.

Inherited Abilities?

I think it's very possible that psychic ability is inherited. My mother would talk openly about spirits and other strange things that would happen to her. She is very religious but also believes in the paranormal. She has visions and strong sensations. My sister and I are clairsentient (a psychic term meaning 'clear-sensing'), and sometimes I get a knowing. I didn't show any psychic ability in my teens because I really wasn't interested and didn't believe in 'that baloney'. Then it all came back in full force when I was about 25. All four of my children show some ability. Two of my kids see things and one is a lot like me. I also believe that the more open you are about your own ability, the more it will show itself.

Paula, on the other hand, is not so sure that the abilities are passed through the family.

> I think the 'inheritance' isn't really inheritance … it just sounds good to the ear! I think we are who we are … I think we all have this capability, but maybe not all of our spirits can handle what comes along with it, and if a parent has this experience, then it is 'safer' emotionally to walk onto this 'path'.
>
> I am psychic and so are my children, ages four and one. I can tell you from my own experience that they both have chosen this path, and if it were not for their parents being open to it, they would have great challenges.
>
> Personally, I believe that it is the parents who must feel safe with it first, because our kids will follow suit.

Auras

Seeing auras (the natural energy field around the body) and their different colours is a common trait of the new psychic children.

The different colours of the aura are said to represent different vibrations or personality traits. Colours can vary throughout the day depending on one's 'mood'. Other colours remain in the aura.

Here is a rough list, although each shade can have different meanings – so don't take this as the *ultimate* list!

Children often see spirits this way, too, so it would be interesting to find out if the same colours of the personality cross over with us living beings!

- **red**: angry, creative, persistent and passionate
- **orange:** thoughtful, motivated, disciplined and courageous
- **yellow:** cheerful, focused, thoughtful and introverted
- **brown**: organized, disciplined, earthly, hard working and sensible
- **green**: spiritual, healing, sociable, inventive and stressed
- **pink:** loving, faithful and unwise
- **blue:** healing, sensitive, intuitive, seeking harmony, principled, safe and psychic
- **purple:** spiritual, industrious, dreaming, humble and psychic
- **grey:** engaging in spiritual practices, connected, guided, on the right path
- **cream:** tuned in, aware
- **black**: angry, ill, traumatized, depressed, trapped, or protected.

Auras need to be read by professionals, really, but this may give you an indication and a place to start if your child sees auras. Your child may be able to give you a more comprehensive list, so it's worth checking out!

If your child sees ghostly spirits of different colours, you can see if the colours 'feel' the same as the ones for living human souls. Ask your child – you might be surprised at what he or she tells you.

Spiritually-inspired Artists

New psychic talents can appear in many ways. Some of these take the form of creative pursuits such as music and art.

Akiane Kramarik is a young artist whose paintings are inspired by God. The young prodigy says that she met God in her cradle as a young baby and that God began showing her visions when she was just four years old. She now translates these visions in her work.

Akiane is a very modest but extremely talented artist with a very mature understanding of the world and why she is here. Born in July, 1994, in Mount Morris, Illinois to an American father and a Lithuanian mother, she believes that God helps her to paint so that her artwork will teach others.

She uses extraordinary colour in her work and talks about there being many more colours than we are able to see on Earth. Her brilliantly lifelike paintings of people have the most amazing eyes. She describes God as a ball of light … she is also a wonderful musician and creates poetry to illustrate her artwork.

Akiane believes that she has been blessed by God for one reason and one reason only: 'to help others'.

This young artist's work has to be seen to be believed. If you want to view Akiane's work (and listen to an interview of Akiane describing her talent), visit www.youtube.com and do a search on her name. There is also an official website: www.akiane.com.

CHAPTER 3

Mediumship: Connecting to the 'Other' Side

Even death is not to be feared by one
who has lived wisely.

Buddha

Contact with the Afterlife

Many young children seem aware of realms of existence
which quite simply baffle us adults. Our young children
are 'mini-mediums', which gives them the ability to see,
feel and hear angels and loved ones from the other side
of life. A 'medium' is a psychic who has the ability to
bridge the gap between our realms and heaven.

Is it because our own dear children have so recently
come from the heavenly realms, being born *from* heaven?
Are children more open to afterlife contact, or perhaps this
ability is stronger now because the human race is growing
and developing (or rediscovering) sixth-sense abilities?

Many believe that the human race is going through a type of transition period and that our children may be advanced souls who are coming to help us during this difficult period of our Earth's history. We certainly need all the help we can get right now. Humankind is doing a poor job of looking after the planet and each other. Wouldn't it be wonderful to think that the souls of our special children had decided to be born at this time to help in some way? I will look at the strange phenomena surrounding this suggestion later in this book.

Certainly more and more children have the extraordinary ability to communicate with the unseen realms of heaven and the spirits who reside there.

Because our loved ones on the other side of life are drawn close to us, on what mediums call 'a love link', innocent children are especially easy to reach. Love acts as a sort of magnet, bringing our deceased loved ones close to us. Children seem more likely to be able to pick up this contact. They're also more likely to take the whole thing in their stride. If the energy is friendly and familiar, they are unlikely to be afraid.

Loved Ones Who Visit from the Other Side

Deceased grandparents, parents and siblings are regular visitors to children on this side of life. They see no need for the family to trouble themselves with a visit to a professional psychic medium; the spirits of our loved ones are most happy appearing to the youngsters in the family by visiting 'direct'.

Be aware if you hear your toddler chatting away to an 'invisible' friend at night-time. The visitor may be invisible to you, but it's highly likely that your child can see – and know – exactly who is visiting!

Margaret Ann knows this only too well. Here is her story.

You See Angel, Mummy?

When my grandmother (who brought me up as her own daughter) passed away on January 6th, my little girl Shelbi really comforted me. As I was sitting on the sofa one night thinking about my grandparents (whom I called Mum and Dad), she came and sat next to me and said, 'Dry your tears away, Mummy. Nana Margaret is with Granddad Jimmy.'

I asked her where they where and she said, 'They're in the green car.' Now, my grandparents used to have a green car and they loved going out for drives.

My dear uncle bought me a pendant with a photo of my grandparents in it. When Shelbi saw it she said right away, 'That's Nana Margaret and Granddad Jimmy, Mummy.'

I said, 'Yes, that's right. Do you see them OK?' and she replied, 'Yes, Mummy, they're sitting on the couch and Granddad Jimmy's eating white sweets.' Rather bizarrely, the night before my granddad passed away my mum (his daughter) gave him a pack of Mint Imperials!

Sadly I lost what would have been my third baby in the womb. My baby's skull had not formed properly and it caused the brain to be exposed. I called this baby Angel. One day Shelbi was looking through a soft toy book that was bought for her a few Christmases ago; it has various Christmas-type things in it. She turned to the page with an angel depicted on it and said, 'You see angel, Mummy?' I said, 'Yes, honey, I do.' She said, 'Look, Jesus fixed her head now. But she's still in the clouds.'

This totally took me aback because this was before I told Shelbi about Angel having a sore head. But she just knew. She also told my little boy James, who is not far off turning two years old, that it's Angel who comes and sings 'Twinkle, Twinkle, Little Star,' but goes before anyone can see her. She tells him that if he wants to see her, he's to look at the clouds!

Shelbi seems to know what she is talking about! Her experience is not frightening at all. How wonderful that even though she missed the experience of her great grandparents and sister Angel in life she is able to connect with them in the afterlife.

Sometimes this ability will stay with the child into adulthood too. Your own reaction as a parent or guardian will likely affect whether this extraordinary power is enhanced or closes down. Margaret Ann is handling it perfectly.

Jade is just 16 and shared her own visitation experience with me.

Nana in a Bright Light

I have always believed in the 'afterlife'. I think reading about different people's stories of their experiences helped. Then I had my own experience ... one I shall never forget.

My nan lived in Suffolk, and me and my family lived down in Surrey. We used to go and visit her occasionally when I had my Easter or summer holidays. It was nice where she lived, very peaceful and surrounded by lovely countryside. She had moved so she could look after her late father, but after he passed away she decided to stay. She believed herself that this world wasn't the only world we live in (and she told me she was going to prove this to me later on!).

Nan believed because she'd had her own experiences. Both her own mum and her nan had visited her whilst she was lying in bed, and Nan had told me all about it.

One day we had some bad news. Nan had cancer. She seemed to cope with it well and never let it get in the way of her life. She then decided that it would be a good idea to move nearer her family, which was good because I then got to spend more time with her!

But then there was more bad news. The cancer had spread and she was diagnosed with 'terminal cancer'.

Near the end she had to be moved into a hospice, where they took very good care of her. She died in January 2007, when I was just 14. It was deeply upsetting, but then Nana kept her promise ...

One night I awoke to see a bright light by my bed-room doorway. Then a figure slowly walked through the white light. I was shocked at first but then I could see it was my nan. She walked a couple more steps towards me and smiled and waved. I had my arm stretched out to try to reach to her. I remember stuttering, 'N-n-nana,' then as she slowly turned away to walk back into the light I blurted out, 'I love you.'

I woke up suddenly with my heart beating fast as though I had been running for 15 minutes! I sat up-right in my bed amazed by what I had just seen. I wasn't scared, just shocked and amazed. It was wonderful!

I know it certainly wasn't a dream because it was too real, but I wasn't fully awake, either. I've read that you have different stages/levels of sleep, and at the start of one of those levels, spirits can enter and visit.

I had another 'dream' shortly afterwards where we were both in a room with just a sofa. We were sitting there with my little niece Leah, who was due to be born the day Nana died. In my dream she was cuddling Leah, and we were having a chat like we used to when Nana was alive!

I had my cat Poppy ever since I was born (I'm 16 now and Poppy was nearly 17 when she died!). She was a tortoiseshell and was known to be a bit snappy, but

Poppy always loved to be around the family. She spent a lot of time in my bedroom, lying on her back on my bed or rug. If she wasn't there she would be in her own bed next to the radiator.

Near the end of her life her kidneys were just failing. Even then she tried to use all her energy to get to my bedroom! It wasn't nice to see her suffer, so we made a family decision to take her to the vet and get him to put her to sleep. Then we buried her in the garden. She has the best place and is surrounded by flowers. I miss her so much.

I asked her a couple of days after she died if she would be able to come and visit me in a dream, just so that I knew she was OK. And she did just that! She was lying on her back in her relaxed cat position, with me stroking her and her saying, 'I'm OK, I'll always be here with you!'

I also had another dream where she was walking up to me on my bed, and I cuddled her. I still do really miss her, and ask her occasionally to visit me whenever she can. In the meantime, whenever I feel down I go to my message board where I have all my pictures of her, in my bedroom – our favourite place to be together!

I feel extremely pleased to have experienced these things, as it has reassured me that we never actually die, just move to a better world where we can meet all the ones we have loved again!

Jade's right! What perfect experiences of loving messages from the other side of life with both humans and animals. Here is Sarah's story.

Be a Good Boy

My mum died in March 2006. Shortly after she passed, my son, who was three at the time, told me that he had seen his nan and she had spoken to him!

I couldn't believe my ears when he said that Nan had said, 'Hello, Danny. I love you and I want you to be a very good boy for your mum and let her get a good night's sleep by staying in your own bed all night.'

When Mum was alive I used to moan about how tired I was all the time because my son kept coming into my room.

Danny told me that his nanny had said she would be proud of him if he slept in his own bed, and then told him that she had to go and look after Granddad.

Danny said that there was a big light up in the sky and Nanny went through it. The next day I phoned my dad and told him what Danny had told me. He said he was probably dreaming … but I'm not so sure.

Danny sounds to me like he had a real visit. All aspects of the experience reflect the afterlife contact stories that people send me from all over the world, including the traditional 'light' which Danny is unlikely to have read about!

Linda's granddad appeared with a guardian spirit.

Stop Crying

When I was young I was very attached to my granddad. I used to tell him everything about my stepmum beating me up from an early age. My dad wouldn't listen to me and used to think I was just trying to cause trouble.

Granddad was always there for me. Then when I was about 15 my granddad took ill and, before I knew it, he died. It came as a real shock and I was totally devastated. I was that bad they called the doctor to ask if he would give me something to calm me down, but the doctor refused and said it would do me good to grieve.

My stepmum said I couldn't go to his funeral just in case I 'showed them up'. I had to stay at my grandma's flat until everyone got back. I will never forget what happened next. I was crying so hard. All I wanted was my granddad. Then I felt a presence and this figure appeared in a long golden gown. He was holding Granddad and lifting him upwards. The being said, 'Stop crying, he's safe and well and will always be with you no matter where you go.'

I was so shocked, I rubbed my eyes. I thought I must have fallen asleep after crying so much, so I nipped myself that hard I cut my hand. To this day I have a little scar which I call my 'Granddad scar'.

Over the years I have noticed a real pattern to these stories of grandparents and great-grandparents. Grandmas are usually the ones that come to say goodbye and reassure, and usually granddads come to protect and watch over our little ones. The message always seems to reflect this: 'Don't worry, I'm always going to be here for you,' or 'I'm your guardian angel now.'

My own father died just a few short weeks ago and has already visited several of his own grandchildren, including one of my teenage daughters …

Why Are You Crying?

I had been having trouble sleeping and after Granddad died I cried a lot during the night. Then one night I had a vivid dream. I dreamt I rang the family on my mobile phone to find out where they were. Mum told me they were all in a restaurant and so I decided to meet them there.

When I arrived at the restaurant I noticed the family were sitting with a man. The man looked a lot like Granddad, so I wondered if this was why he was with them. I knew that Granddad had died.

As I got closer I realized that the man *was* Granddad and he asked me for a hug. I actually felt his arms around me.

Then the scene changed. Granddad and I were sitting on a boat in the middle of a lake. I told Granddad that I must trust him a lot to sit backwards in a boat because I was so frightened of the water. I had told him this shortly before he died. I noticed that older male family members were standing on the bank. It was as if they were there to reassure me.

Granddad then showed me how he died. He had one sharp pain in his chest, then just lifted out of his body. The next thing he remembers is waking up on the other side.

He asked me why I was crying and reassured me that he was fine and hadn't gone far away. Afterwards I saw Nanny, who is still alive. She was standing on the side of the bank and told me, 'We must tell everyone that Granddad is OK.' Then my boyfriend came to collect me and we drove off together.

Strangely enough, my daughter's boyfriend also had an unusual dream experience with 'Granddad', whom he had met just a couple of times. Both of them were sitting on the side of a lake with a setting sun, and he told me, 'The sky was filled with the most beautiful colours I have ever seen in my life.' The two of them had a discussion about fishing before my dad got up to walk away. He turned back and said, 'Take good care of her.'

I think Dad was checking out his granddaughter's boyfriend! I figure he passed the test!

Linda's story:

Magpies

Since my mum passed in August 2000 I have constantly tried to reach her in some way. One day I asked her to give me a sign to show me that she was still around and could hear me. As she loved birds, I asked her to show me five magpies together. I know you often see two or three, but I thought that five was a good number to ask for as proof.

All the next day I kept my eyes open for the magpies, but didn't see even one. As I went to pick up my daughter from the stables I remember feeling very disappointed. On the way home my daughter was chatting away about her day with her pony when she said something that made me prick up my ears. 'Oh, guess what I saw today, Mum. Five magpies outside Comet's stable!'

I couldn't help smiling and feeling very excited too! That was about five years ago. Recently my other daughter was in hospital with severe stomach pains and the doctors decided to keep her in overnight. My other daughter and I went to visit her, and on the way out of the hospital she asked Grandma to keep an eye on her sister and make her well quickly. She remembered the magpies and asked for the same sign.

As we walked out of the main doors of the hospital there was a flock of magpies in a tree, and as we passed they all took flight ... all but five, that is! Now if that's not proof, then I don't know what is.

Here is Laura's story.

Brother Visits

I have always found angels very interesting, but wasn't sure if I really believed in them until September 2005 when I was expecting my second child (I already had a daughter, Ellen, who was four). My second child was going to be a boy and I had a problem-free pregnancy, but it all went wrong when I was 42 weeks along. Tragically, my son Andrew died during labour.

I truly believe he is our angel now, as so many strange things have happened to us since then, some of which I cannot explain.

My daughter took his death hard and I remember her waking one night in tears. She was very upset with me and she said accusingly, 'You told me I wouldn't be able to see Andrew any more.' I told her that was right, we would never see Andrew again. Her reply was, 'Then why is he playing in the tree at the bottom of the garden?'

After a few weeks, when my husband returned to work, he fell asleep at the wheel of his car. All of a sudden he felt a very cold blast of air and was immediately wide awake again. We can't explain it but he feels that someone was watching over him that day.

I myself had a very weird dream one night. I dreamt that my husband, Andrew, Ellen and myself were all in bed. In the dream Andrew was taken from me. He was found in a beautiful white castle. He had blond hair (he had very dark hair when he left us) and was wearing a white babygro. He told me in the dream that he was very happy and I was not to be sad. When I woke up I felt very calm and couldn't understand why I was so happy in the dream. I still missed my baby so much, but felt very comforted by the experience. When I woke up the next morning I found a single white feather by the side of my bed.

Three months later I fell pregnant with my third child. I was very stressed and worried about the new baby, which was also another boy. He was due one year and three days after Andrew died, and I had regular nightmares about the same thing happening to my new baby. I didn't tell Ellen until I was 27 weeks along. Imagine my surprise when I did tell her. She seemed to know already and said, 'I know, Mum, it's another boy. Andrew told me!' We were all so surprised – and it turned out she was right.

When I got to about 27 weeks I dreamt that Oliver (the name we had picked for the new baby) would be stillborn in August. The dream was so clear and very scary. I dreaded entering the month of August. I was so sure it was all going to go wrong again.

When I went for my scan at 32 weeks, the doctors told us Oliver had problems with his kidneys. The condition should have been picked up at about 16 weeks, and even though I'd already had 12 scans before that, nothing appeared wrong up until that point. Did Andrew know I wanted Oliver here before August?

Oliver was born by caesarean section at 34 weeks on the 3rd of August 2006, 11 months to the day after losing Andrew. Luckily his kidneys were not as bad as we expected and he surprised all the doctors. He had an operation at a week old. I still cannot explain how a feather got into Oliver's clothes when he was on the eighth floor of the hospital!

Oliver is now 17 months old and doing very well. His consultant said he was a very lucky boy, and that normally boys with this condition have lifelong problems. I guess his brother is helping him still! We always seem to find a feather when we ask Andrew to watch over us, and Oliver is regularly found laughing at a particular spot on the wall. As for Ellen, she is always talking, playing and laughing with her late brother. It's wonderful to know that he is still around us all.

Isn't it amazing how children have this ability? This next story was sent to me by Catrina. Her daughter Karen seems to have a direct line to relatives on the other side of life.

Chatting to the Witch?

When I was going through a messy divorce, my daughter was just a toddler. We were driving through the snow one day when a lorry pulled out in front of us. My mum and daughter were in the car with me and I hadn't long passed my driving test, so it was a big challenge! How I managed to avoid that lorry and the railings was beyond me, but I was very relieved and glad I did. A few minutes later and almost home, my daughter was chattering away to herself and she said, 'It's OK, I'm chatting to the witch who helped us!' You can imagine we were intrigued!

Mum and I had an idea of whom she might have meant, so when we got to Mum's we took a photograph out and set it on the table. My daughter recognized it immediately and started shouting, 'That's the witch in the car!' It was my great-grandmother, and I guess to a kid her hair did look like a witch's!

Later we had another weird experience. I was beginning to get distressed about the delays in my divorce, and again we were at my mum's and stepdad's house. My aunt and uncle were visiting and Karen was playing behind a chair, chattering away to herself. My aunt asked me how the court case was going when suddenly Karen blurted out, 'Mum, don't worry, Peggy and Wullie are with you.' We all just sat agog, as nobody apart from close friends ever called my gran and granddad that, not even my mum! Had Peggy and Wullie been with us in the room?

It just goes to show that when you are struggling there's always someone looking out for you.

There is indeed! Now here's Helma's account. Helma is from the Netherlands and writes about her deceased son, Remy.

Another Brother Visits

Remy was my eldest son. He was stillborn in 1987 after a pregnancy from 29 weeks. My husband and I had a hard time after we lost him.

Then in 1988 our son Timo was born. He didn't sleep through the night until he was four years old. Several times when I walked into his room he was lying awake and he told me that there was a little man in his room. I took it seriously because I also had been visited by deceased family members over the years. Sometimes I felt their experience and sometimes I had seen coloured lights around me, but I never found it frightening.

Two years ago I made a drawing of special things that had belonged to every part of my family. When I showed that drawing to Timo he looked at the part of the drawing that stood for Remy and he said to me, 'Mum, that's the little man I saw in my room when I was small.'

Brothers and sisters seem to retain their connection even if one passes over to the other side.

Here's another story relating to a grandparent. Dawn's experience was very vivid even though she was so young. She's never forgotten it.

Great-grandma Ghost?

I must have been around three years old when I saw a woman in white smiling at me from the top of my grandparents' stairs. After seeing her three or four times I asked my mother who she was. Mum told me that there was no one else in the house, but I was so convinced that I dragged my mother round upstairs to try and find the woman. We found no one.

I never saw this woman again but never forgot about her even though I felt cheated when I realized I couldn't actually prove that I had seen her.

Then recently I discovered that my great-grand-mother used to live in that very house and had recently died when I saw my vision. Although I don't remember her in life I wondered if it had been my great-grandma visiting me!

Jessica, too, remembers her own experience vividly – even though she was very young!

Saying Goodbye

When I was two I lived at my grandparents' house with my mum, grandma, granddad and great-nana. I was very close to my great-nana, who used to play with me during the day while everyone else was busy. When she died suddenly, my mum came to break the news to me gently whilst I was playing in my cot.

'Jess, I have something to tell you, sweetheart,' she started.

'Oh, it's OK, Mummy, I know. Great-nana has gone to heaven now. She came past the window in an aero-plane and waved goodbye to me.'

My mum was astounded.

Holly lost her dad back in March. She tells me that her dad and her oldest son were extremely close.

Invisible Hands

My son had a visit from his uncle, my brother, who died six years ago. My brother told my son that he had arrived to collect Papaw, my dad. My son even told me what day his granddad was going to pass. My son was right. I rang him from the hospital to tell him that Papaw had died and he already knew.

My son tells me all the time he misses his Papaw, but today was different. Today I came home from work and he ran out to the garage to greet me. He was crying and telling me he was sad, and when I asked him why he said, 'Because he moved out.'

I asked who had moved out, and he told me *Papaw*. It was the first time I had seen him cry since my dad passed away. He told me how Papaw had been here right after he passed away, but that he had now left. Then my son told me that when he fell off the bed earlier in the day, someone saved him and he felt invisible hands!

I'm sure that Papaw hasn't gone far away!

Children Who Visit from the Other Side of Life

June shares her very sad … and happy story.

Cup of Tea

I lost my son in a car accident, when he was aged 17. Two weeks after the accident I saw him passing my bedroom!

63

He was wearing a T-shirt and shorts, which he normally wore to bed, and he asked me if I wanted a cup of tea.

A few months later, he came to me in my sleep. Usually when I dream, things aren't right – I know I am in my own house, or who the people are I am talking to, but they always look different. When my son appeared in my dream, everything was right. All the furniture in my house was in the place it normally is, for example. I asked him for a cuddle and he ran into his own room (which he would normally do, not wanting Mum to cuddle him). I ran after him and gave him a cuddle and it felt so real. This wasn't an ordinary dream!

No one can convince me that there isn't a life after we pass. I believe we don't die; there is no such thing. We just shed our earthly coat.

Loved Ones as Guardian Angels

Many times our loved ones on the other side of life tell their loving grandchildren, children and siblings that they are their 'guardian angel'.

Although maybe not angels in the traditional sense, they do seem able to pop back and keep an eye on things. It's almost as if they have an insight into what is going on in our lives, maybe even seeing a little way ahead in time – but don't worry, they don't follow you around all the time … they totally respect privacy! (Phew.)

After Jeanette's daughter described her visitor, Jeanette felt that it was her husband's brother – her daughter's uncle. Jeanette explains.

Night-time Protection

My daughter is 14 years old and she woke one night to find a spirit man sitting in her room. She was shocked at first, but he sat there and just smiled. She said each night she would speak to the spirit and just say, 'Good night, man in my room,' and each night she would dream and he would be in her dream, always smiling and waving.

She told me she wasn't scared, and then one night she asked if he had a message for her. He replied in a very deep voice that he had no message but that he was just there to look after her.

Many people would call these human-looking guardians 'spirit guides'. Our spirit guide's role is to keep us on our life path … to ensure that we follow the life plan we decided upon before birth. Our spirit guides, like our own dear family on the other side of life, love us totally. Many believe that the same spirit guides help us in all of our lives, so they are very dear friends who know us very well. This idea fits in very well with my own beliefs. What about you?

Angie's daughter Erin was able to see family visitors from the afterlife and knows that she is being watched over because they told her so.

Taking Care of Us

Last year, not that long after my mum passed away, I woke up in the early hours of the morning and heard my daughter Erin speaking to someone. When I asked her whom she was chatting to, she said that she was speaking to Ma (that's what she called her grandmother). I told her to go back to sleep and not to be frightened, as Ma was just looking after her and taking care of all of us. Erin wasn't the least bothered by it and explained, 'I know, Mummy, that's what she said to me!' It reminded me of several years earlier when Erin was just over a year old. She kept on staring into the hall and saying that 'the man' was there. When we went down to my mum and dad's house, she pointed to a picture of my brother who had passed away before Erin was born. She seemed to know him and we guessed he must have been the mystery visitor!

There are more of these wonderful protection and 'guardian angel' stories in the next chapter.

Handling the Visits Properly for Well-balanced Children

During less enlightened times, youngsters were scolded and punished for their talents. It was a rare adult who even believed the child, and I'm sad to say that I do get occasional letters from psychic adults who were smacked and locked in their rooms for 'lying' about seeing ghosts and spirits when they were children!

Fear can make people do extraordinary things – both good and bad. These adults still bear the emotional scars. Lindsay remembers only too well.

Told Off

I always knew from a young age that there was something else apart from this life. I don't recall how I knew, I just did.

My first encounter was with my late granddad, who had died a short time before. I saw him sat on the end of his bed, looking in the mirror and doing up his tie, quite normally.

He turned and smiled at me, and I promptly ran down the stairs four at a time because I was so excited. Sadly, no one believed me. I was eight years old, and was promptly told off for upsetting my nan by 'making up' stories!

Angie had the same problem. She explains:

Shunned

I sometimes wonder what I would be like if I had been able to have my abilities nurtured when I was a young girl. My mom had to keep me quiet because my dad would have thrown a 'royal fit'!

The funny thing now, though, is that he knows about my own daughter's psychic abilities and doesn't shun her about it. (He only knows she can heal, though, and nothing else. I think if he knew more it might scare him!)

Reactions of Other Children

Children can have difficulties with their gifts as they get older ... especially if they have to fight convention. Their gifts might not be a problem at pre-school age or infant school, because many children use their power of 'imagination' in games and may not realize that their 'invisible' friends are real.

One woman told me, 'My daughter is six. She embraces her gifts at the moment. She doesn't feel different from other children; however, other children don't understand when she talks about things they can't see or hear.'

Why Do the Spirits Come?

So why do our loved ones visit? If you were a grandparent who missed the birth of a grandchild ... and you could come back for a visit, wouldn't you? Of course! Relatives on the other side of life are just as interested in the children and grandchildren they have yet to meet as any of us would be. Incidentally, they don't lose interest at 18, either, and if they are still able to visit they will just as likely turn up at school award ceremonies, or on the day you pass your driving test, or at your engagement and your wedding!

Older relatives will sometimes come to say goodbye to the children they loved on the earthly plane, or they will warn them their passing is imminent by visiting in dreams in the hours before their spirit leaves the physical body (like the grandma waving goodbye from a plane!). Naturally not wanting the children to be frightened, they prefer to explain to the child themselves that they are going to the heavenly realms.

Nicola remembers:

Goodbye Light ...

After my gran had been in hospital for two weeks, my little cousin, aged seven, told us about his dream experience. He asked his mother, 'Is Gran going to die, because last night in my dream she was walking towards a big bright light?'

Nicola's gran did die, just three short weeks later, but it seems as if her spirit already had one foot in heaven!

People can often see their own passed-over loved ones in the days and weeks before they, too, pass over, and as Gran's spirit was loosening in her own physical body, she was able to show this to her grandson, even if he might not have been totally sure of the meaning of the visit at the time.

Incidentally, Gran visited her elder grandchild Nicola, too, just as she was leaving the body. Nicola recalls:

I'm OK, Be Strong

On the Thursday night I went to my bed and I can remember the 'dream' I had as it was so clear and the emotions I felt were very real. I was running up the hospital corridor but by the time I got outside her room the nurse told me that I was too late and that she had passed away already.

She asked me if I wanted to go in and say goodbye, so I did. But when I went in she was sitting up looking quite her normal self. I was so confused and kept muttering, 'What's going on? I don't understand!' Then Gran said to me, 'Nicola, I don't want you to worry, everything will be OK. I'm OK and you have to be strong and tell everyone I love them.' The last thing she said to me was, 'Oh, and you will dance.' I am a competitive freestyle dancer, and the week before Gran died I told my mum I wasn't going to the European championships if anything happened to Gran. I believe Gran was telling me that she wanted me to go!

I was woken up by the phone ringing. It was my mum ringing to tell me that my gran's breathing had deteriorated and they were on their way to the hospital. They didn't make it, but Gran had already been to say goodbye to me, so I felt at peace.

I often cry when I read these amazing stories. They remind me of the loss of my own loved ones, but the stories are comforting and I believe these extraordinary experiences are for us all to share. Life does go on.

I have also heard other stories where children seem to know things that adults don't. Are children just more perceptive? Or is it their psychic abilities which lead the way? Here's another story for you to consider.

Don't Cry

My mother passed away two years ago. My daughter, who we have always known had a sensitive side, knew that Gran was poorly and that doctors couldn't make her better. She told us, 'Gran is going to heaven, Mam, so she'll be OK again.'

I never said any more to her because, to be honest, I was a little taken aback by her comment. Sadly, Mam did pass just a week later and my daughter caught me crying on my own. She was concerned and said, 'Don't cry, Mam, Gran is OK now.' I told my daughter that I was sad because I missed Gran so much and wanted to tell her that.

My daughter, so wise beyond her years, said, 'She said she knows, Mam, she is sitting next to you!' Of course, I turned around but couldn't see anything.

My daughter continued, 'You mustn't be sad and cry any more because she is happy and is better again.' I did cry more, though, because I wanted to see her, too.

Every week I went to visit my mam's grave. Then I had to have a major operation to replace my hip. When I came out of hospital I was feeling sorry for myself because I knew I was not well enough to visit the grave. My daughter put me right, though, and asked me, 'Why do you need to go there to visit Gran when she is here?'

I am sure my daughter is right. Even though I can't see her, I believe my daughter can. She talks to her gran on a regular basis, which is so lovely. I do hope she never loses her special ability.

Watching Us Live

Our loved ones often make an appearance to let us know that they are aware of our achievements. Many adults who lost their parents when they were younger ask me, 'Do my parents know what I have achieved in life? Are they proud of me?'

Naturally our loved ones like to reach out to us when they can and reassure us that they keep an eye on this side of life and like to offer their support. Of course they are proud of you!

Here is Linda and her daughter's experience.

Charity Race

My father-in-law passed away in February this year. He had cancer. We have two young children and our daughter took the news very badly. At 11 years old, she was very close to her granddad.

One night I saw the Race for Life advertised on TV. You may be aware that this is a race run by women to raise money for Cancer Research. I thought this might give our daughter something to aim for and help her deal with her feelings, so I booked for the two of us to run.

We ran in the pouring rain but had a fabulous time. At the end of the day we felt very proud of ourselves. The whole day was a very emotional one.

When we completed the race, my husband and younger son were waiting for us at the finishing line. My husband had my mobile phone in his pocket and I asked him for it so that I could text everyone and let them know how we'd got on. As he took the phone out of his pocket it had gone straight to the name DAD and his phone number (I had not yet deleted him from my phone). It was amazing to feel that he might be trying to reach out to us and we all cried. It was just as if Dad were standing with us, telling us how proud he was of us both.

Since reading your book *Angels Watching Over Me* (which touched me greatly), I have had many experiences that confirm to me that I have an angel watching over me too.

Thanks, Linda! I'm glad my book was comforting! I, too, have kept my dad's number programmed into my mobile phone. Perhaps one day he will 'ring' me too.

This next experience is from Hannah, who is just 13 years old. Hannah also wrote to me after reading *Angels Watching Over Me*.

Pleased to Meet You

I've had many paranormal experiences even though I'm still young. I usually share my experiences with my nana because I know she's had many experiences, too. Since my mum read your book she now understands this and it has helped a lot.

My granddad Alan was my dad's father and I never got to meet him because he died of a heart attack when my dad was around his mid-twenties. Even my mum never got to meet him, but my nana was kind enough to give me a photo of him (with my cousin Mark as a baby), so now I remember him by that.

I used to get really upset and sometimes still do because everyone says he was such a lovely man. I felt sad because I never got to meet this wonderful man.

But then one night he came to me in a dream. In the dream, all of my family were at my auntie Karen's for a house party (Karen is Alan's eldest daughter). This dream was sort of weird, though, because it was almost as if I was going back in time. I remember seeing my granddad wearing his favourite navy jumper and holding cousin Mark as a baby in an armchair. I found this weird because this is the setting of my special photograph of him.

> Granddad beckoned me over, so I walked over and gave him a hug and sat on the arm of the chair. I was surprised and said to him, 'Granddad, what are you doing here?'
>
> 'I've come to see you,' he told me. I asked him why and he explained, 'You need to stop worrying yourself – just because we never met in life doesn't mean I don't love you! You're my granddaughter and I love you just the same as all the others and you need to remember that.'
>
> I was so happy and thanked him and gave him a hug, while he just laughed. Just as he was about to leave, he said, 'If you ever need me I'm always around. Just give me a shout, OK?' And then he went.

I love that Hannah's granddad created a 'meeting scenario' that he felt she would feel comfortable with. It's not unknown for spirits to take us to places we used to know, wear familiar clothes and bring in other familiar family members (both living and dead). In one of the stories I recount in *Angels Watching Over Me*, the granddad even wore his earthly glasses (even though he no longer needed them on the heavenly plane) so that his granddaughter would recognize him!

Some of the experiences in *Angels Watching Over Me* are about the youngsters in families who are already in their heavenly home. Many parents, brothers and sisters see these spirit children in dreams and visions, and the spirit children sometimes leave other little signs that they are around us still.

Yesterday I was working my way through my post-bag of readers' letters and questions (I am always behind with my post). I had just opened another batch and had around 100 letters piled up beside me. It usually takes me around 20 minutes or so to answer each one, so I normally try and get through half a dozen each day (and when the pile gets too high, my PA Debbie helps out and is assisted by my dear mother … thanks, Mum!).

Sometimes the letters are very sad and make me cry. Other times the stories people share are miraculous and life-changing. I love receiving them all. Yesterday's batch of letters was a real mixture as usual.

When I went to bed (late) I fell asleep facing the centre of the bed. Normally I face outwards (easier to avoid my husband's snoring! No doubt if he reads this he will tell you my snoring's even louder!).

I hadn't been asleep long when someone poked me hard in the back! I woke up and spun around. A little spirit girl was standing by my bed. She was beautiful and I knew immediately she belonged to one of the families whose letter I had replied to earlier in the day.

Sadly, as I tried to focus on her she immediately faded out of sight and I didn't get the chance to talk to her. It was exciting to see my little spirit visitor just the same. I immediately woke my husband to tell him what had happened (although to be fair, he was only vaguely interested – it was the middle of the night, after all!).

This is only the third time that the spirit of someone I don't know has visited me in such a visual way, so this was a special moment for me. I immediately rushed downstairs to locate my reply to the reader's letter I had written earlier in the day. I tore open the envelope so that I could share my experience with the family. Their little girl was alive and well – just in another place, and she had been to visit me! I hope they didn't think I was crazy!

How clever are these kids? This little girl had travelled through time and space to connect with someone she didn't know because she realized that here was someone who could reassure her family that she was safe and well! Awesome! More brilliant stories like this in later chapters.

CHAPTER 4

Angels Watching Over Children

Let the little children come to me, and do not hinder
them, for the kingdom of God belongs to such as these.

Mark 10:14

During the course of my work I often read stories about
children whose lives were saved by unseen beings (angels? spirits?) … and actually, sometimes by 'beings' who
were not 'unseen', but very much visible to the children
they have helped!

When children see angels, they tend to get the 'full
works': glowing white figures with wings. The right angel appears for the job. When the child is in danger, they
are more likely to see a warrior type of angel (someone
strong who can protect them from danger); in situations
where healing or nursing is needed, the child tends to
see an angel of female gender (showing caring energies).
Naturally angels, as beings of light, don't need bodies

at all – so the 'façade' of a comforting-looking figure is for the children's benefit, to calm them when they are in need.

On other occasions the 'angel' is a departed relative, sometimes one who is familiar to the child, at other times unknown (although the children are able to pick people out when they are shown family photographs). I have many stories where the grandfather is the 'angel'. Granddads have been very important in the caring role.

Tanya comes from Dubai and she has never forgotten her encounter with a saviour from the other side of life.

Granddad Plays 'Catch'

I was only about eight years old when my grandfather died. I found it so hard not to cry every time somebody reminded me of him.

Late one afternoon, a couple of months after his death, my cousin and I were playing in the backyard climbing trees. We were high up in the tree top when a strong wind blew and made me lose my balance, and I went plummeting to the earth below.

As my head was about to hit the ground I desperately tried to reach out for something just to keep me from falling. I was amazed when a figure appeared by a branch and reached for me. It was nothing like I've ever seen in my life before. The figure was not clear, yet I could see the image of his hand reaching out to save me from hitting my head on the ground. The hand pulled me up in a way that, instead of my head crashing down, I actually landed on my feet. My shocked cousin couldn't believe what she had seen, because out of thin air she just saw me being pulled upwards although she didn't see the hand like I had.

When I was safely on the ground, I started to laugh. My cousin asked if I was hurt, but as weird as it may seem I felt amazing. It was as if I had landed on thick clouds rather than the hard ground. I didn't have a single scratch on my body. I told her what I had seen as I fell, and right away we both thought it was my grandfather who had saved me from that fall.

This was just the beginning; since that day I've had many other experiences both from my mother's dad, my father's dad and an aunt, too. They all visit me in dreams when I feel sad. Sometimes I wake up in the middle of the night because of the smell of flowers over my head, and sometimes I see a light 'opening' above me.

I must admit that I am afraid when the lights have opened, but the scent of fresh flowers and the feeling of their love always make me feel safe and protected.

Here's another experience.

Babysitter Angel?

Since my son was a baby I always knew that he was very different from other babies. As he grew I noticed odd behaviours. Although he played by himself, he acted as if he was not alone. I assumed that he had an 'imaginary' friend like you hear people talking about.

One day when he was three years old I took him to visit my husband's uncle's grave. Uncle died when my son was just six weeks old and he never saw my son … As we walked to the grave, my son looked at me and said excitedly, 'Oh, there is Uncle John!' I almost fainted when he said that because I had no idea that he knew anything about his uncle John.

It was then that my son told me about how his uncle John used to visit him and that Uncle John would sit on the moon at night and wave to him. I was stunned.

About a year later my son came to me once again and asked me to tell him about his brother. He was a twin but his twin never developed. Once again, no one had ever told him about this because we always felt he was too young, but he seemed to know about his brother just the same.

He is now 11 years old and has had contact with many different people from the afterlife, including some he doesn't know. He has other abilities, too. All he has to do is look at someone and he will tell me if they have a spirit with them, and then he can describe the spirit to that person.

My son attracts spirits everywhere we go; all I can do is question my son and see if we can find out who they are or what they want.

I keep hearing different things about this talent. After much research on this subject, I have come to the conclusion that God has given my son a very special gift, and it is my job to teach him how to use it in the right way. Through my son I have received many messages from friends on the other side and been lucky enough to have witnessed some remarkable phenomena.

I think that this mum has got it right. A gift from God – I like that!

This next story sounds like another 'angel babysitter' story. Sarah tells me that little Kaitlyn was just three weeks old when her great-grandfather paid a visit.

Misty Visitor Smells of Humbugs

I had just given Kaitlyn a feed and settled her down in the carrycot for a sleep before walking into the kitchen to do the washing-up and make myself something to eat. After a few minutes Kaitlyn started crying, so I turned to dry my hands and go back into the lounge to put her dummy in; which was at the foot of the carrycot.

When I walked into the lounge there was a strong smell of mint humbugs, and a haze around the carrycot. My daughter's dummy was now in her mouth! Kaitlyn could clearly see something and was looking towards the door in the direction of the stairs. She was now calm, and soon after the smell went and so did the haze.

I believe the mystery visitor was my grandfather. He was a big humbug fan and kept them in a special glass sweet jar on the unit in the lounge by his chair. I am glad that he got to see his great-granddaughter and I know that he is always going to look after her wherever I am or wherever I move to.

I'm sure he will!

This is another story of a relative keeping watch from the other side. This story was submitted by Misty, who lives in the southern US.

Daddy Pop

My son Jeremy, who is three years old, was alone in his room watching television. I heard him talking and thought he was just playing or reciting lines from the movie he was watching. Later he walked into the living room, where I was folding clothes, and told me, 'Daddy Pop said to tell Daddy to stop spanking me.' I was thinking to myself, 'You have only had one spanking in your life,' but I suddenly caught on to what he had said. Daddy Pop (great-granddad) had been dead for 28 years.

Jeremy had never met Daddy Pop and the family never really talked about him, so I was surprised, to say the least. I got a strange feeling and asked him what Daddy Pop's real name was, and right away he told me Albert.

I started to feel a little better, because I knew from my husband that Daddy Pop's name was George. I shook it off and told my husband later what had happened. I told him that Jeremy had said Daddy Pop's name was Albert. My husband went quiet and said that part of his family from Georgia called Daddy Pop Albert, which was his middle name. I was still a little sceptical, so I let it go.

Recently we moved into my husband's great-grandmother's house. She had moved to a nursing home. She and Daddy Pop had lived in the house for years before he died. One day my son was playing in his room with his sister Gracie and I heard him laughing. I guessed they were just playing.

Jeremy walked into the dining room and told me that Daddy Pop had visited again and told him he was now a big boy. I looked at him quizzically and I could tell right away that he was serious. This time I just smiled and told him that Daddy Pop was right, he was a big boy now. We were potty-training and he was doing great. He then told me that Daddy Pop was funny and he was going back to talk to him. I said OK.

Later that day I called my husband's grandmother (Daddy Pop's daughter). I shared Jeremy's experiences and wanted to know a little more about this visitor! She suggested I search out an old photograph of him. Actually I found several old photographs of different family members and laid them out on the table. Jeremy picked out Daddy Pop without any problem whatsoever, so now I'm not sure what to think!

Now he tells me all the time that Daddy Pop said this and Daddy Pop said that. Maybe he *is* talking to Daddy Pop, I don't know.

… Maybe he is, Misty, maybe he is! It certainly seems likely to me!

Here is Jo's story.

An Answered Request?

Last weekend we were woken up around four a.m. by music playing on my baby daughter's monitor. We instantly recognized it as being a toy radio in her room. We were confused because you have to turn the dial to make it play the tune, so who could have turned the dial?

As we listened it changed tune, so my husband went in her room. As soon as he opened the door, the music stopped.

It wasn't until later that day that my husband admitted to me that he had asked in his head for his mum to appear to him. My husband is a sceptic still, but I'm sure it was his mum answering his request!

Here is yet another grandfather 'angel' story! This one is from Jayne.

Hospital Visitor

My little boy Sam had a difficult start in life due to severe life-threatening allergies. At the age of three he had severe problems with his elbow and had to have an operation. Terrifyingly, he collapsed under the anaesthetic and had to be resuscitated on more than one occasion due to his reaction to the anaesthetics. It really was a very frightening time. The doctors were concerned that he was in septic shock and thought that they would have to amputate his arm!

When Sam woke from his second operation, he turned to me and said, 'Mummy, it's OK, an old man with funny hair and a yellow dog looked after me. The man said to me, "Come here, Sam, and sit with me and wait a while."'

My mother and my sister were there at the time, and we all just looked at each other knowing exactly whom he had described, but nobody said any more. Luckily Sam made a full recovery and after a six-week stay in hospital he was well enough to return home.

One day we were looking through some old family photographs when Sam got very excited and turned to me and said, 'That's the man, Mum, that's the man who looked after me in hospital, and that's the dog.' Sam had identified my late grandfather and the golden Labrador that I had grown up with.

My grandfather was certainly looking out for him on that occasion, there is no doubt in my mind.

Granddads visit their grandchildren whatever their age, and continue to appear for all special family occasions. He's another wonderful experience.

Granddad the 'Midwife'

At the age of eight and a half I saw my grandpa at the top of our stairs, which scared the wits out of me as he had passed away about six months earlier. I saw him fully dressed and wearing his trilby hat. I could see him clearly but could also see *through* him, which I think is what freaked me out.

I read a story in one of your books that made me realize that what I saw was real. My parents thought I was imagining it.

My granddad Gordon, Gramps as I liked to call him, sadly passed a couple of weeks before my son Matthew was born. When I was in the delivery suite my midwife had gone for a snack and a cup of tea, saying I would be in labour until about three a.m. It was 11 p.m., so I was quite happily settled on the bed, but in no time at all I wanted to push the baby out. My baby certainly wasn't going to wait for the midwife to come back!

Just as my other half went to push the buzzer, my midwife came in. The poor woman only just got her gloves on as my son was born, but because he was born so quickly he wasn't breathing.

The midwife was scrubbing his back to stimulate this and my hubby was looking worried, but I was smiling and really happy and warm. The whole atmosphere in the room changed. It felt like the room was glowing and I knew my gramps was there and I knew he was not alone.

If that room could have been a colour, I would have put money on it being orange. I was so happy and it was amazing to know that my relatives were there to witness my son arrive in this world.

Years later I had a psychic reading and was told that Gramps and his mother were at Matthew's birth, which was lovely for me to hear as confirmation of what I'd felt at the time.

I bet Matthew's great-granddad has a special connection to his grandson. This next story is about a special aunt, and was sent to me by Fiona.

Aunty Announces Birth

On several different occasions I've had a dream about an aunt who had passed away in 1997. She was a heavy drinker and died of an alcohol-related illness. Because of this she always looked painfully thin and grey, and she didn't take care of her appearance at all.

Aunt Margaret was the life and soul of any party; always first up to dance and always last off the dance floor. As the disease took hold over a long period of time, Margaret began to become depressed and not herself at all; she even stopped hiding the fact she was drinking.

Almost five years after she died she came to me in a dream to tell me I was expecting, even before I knew it myself.

I dreamt I was in a dark room and she was sitting high up in a big wooden chair looking down on me. She was laughing her head off, really laughing, and it took ages for her to calm down. Eventually she looked at me and simply said, 'You are going to have a baby and it will be another boy.' Sure enough, I went on to have a boy nine months later!

The next time I dreamt of her, she was holding my hands and smiling. She looked at me for a long time and just said, 'She is on her way.' When I woke up I figured it was just a bizarre dream and thought nothing of it, but I had a much-wanted baby daughter nine months later!

The last time she visited me she looked beautiful. She had make-up on, her hair was done and she had a really beautiful suit on; she looked so healthy. Aunty told me I was to tell the family she had visited and that I was to tell them she was OK. In the dream we were at a family party.

Although Fiona is an adult here, I thought it was relevant that her aunt had announced the birth of her son and daughter. Many believe that our loved ones on the other side can see ahead of time into our future, maybe even knowing the souls of our new young ones before they are born. It's an interesting thought, isn't it?

Here is another experience … another guardian-angel pop!

Guardian-angel Pop

My experience happened many years ago when I lived in London and my youngest son was about 18 months old. The downstairs of our house was all open-plan, with archways instead of doors. The staircase went up from the front of the house, with walls on either side. My son was playing with some cars on the floor when the phone rang (in the lounge).

I went to answer it and a chatty friend was on the phone (causing me problems ending the call). By this time my son had disappeared and I was getting worried because we had no baby gate on the stairs!

Then I heard him fall. It seemed to take the longest time and he must have hit every stair on the way down. Then there was nothing ... just a big empty silence!

My heart missed a beat as I dropped the phone and ran through the dining room and out into the hall. I was really expecting to see my son lying injured on the floor, but no! He was sitting on the bottom stair, swinging his little legs and still holding his car in his hand.

Walking very slowly towards the front door was an old man with his braces hanging down the sides of his trousers and his shirt collar tucked in, just like my granddad 'Pop' used to do. He looked just like my mum's late father when he was getting ready for a wash! Then the man completely vanished before he reached the door. I remember the hall feeling really cold for a few seconds! My son hadn't seen his guardian angel ... but I certainly had!

Jenni comes from Finland and sent me her story in an email:

My Daughter Sees Angels

In one of your books you suggested asking your children about their guardian angels; one day I did just that.

I asked my five-year-old daughter if she had ever seen an angel. I truly expected to get a 'No' and I felt silly even asking. But to my surprise she said, 'Yes,' right away. She began telling me about an angel she saw once when we were visiting a zoo. She was four years old and could remember details like my mother being with us at the zoo and her little brother being asleep in the pram.

She told me how the angel had appeared at her side when we were looking at the rabbits. She explained that the angel was a girl of about her age, with blonde hair and wings, and that the angel smiled at her. The angel stayed by her side for a while and then flew up in the air and circled behind her.

Now, I couldn't believe what I was hearing, but when I started to think about it, it made sense. I too remembered the whole situation (it wasn't so long ago). I remembered standing behind my daughter and looking at her, while she was obviously very surprised and even startled about something she saw to her right. I thought she was looking at an animal, but I couldn't understand where she was looking.

I remember asking her, 'What's the matter, honey? What are you looking at?' And she didn't utter a word. So I asked again, louder, and she looked at me briefly, then looked back to her right, then she suddenly looked up behind her, to the sky, turning her head quickly many times. I looked in the same direction and thought she was looking at a bird or something, but I couldn't see anything. She didn't tell me what it was at the time.

I asked her why she hadn't told me right away. She said that she thought it was a secret as no one else saw the angel.

She has seen angels many times since that first occasion! She told me how an angel appeared to her when she was playing alone in the sandbox in our backyard while I was inside putting her little brother to sleep. She called this the 'mother angel', which I understand means that the angel appeared as a woman. Then she told me about a time when she saw an angel while she was running around with her friends around the playground in front of our house. She also saw an angel stood behind our neighbour's boy (a six-year-old) in the playground and she told him about it, but he could not see anything. On another occasion an angel went through our window!

One day last month we bought her a sleigh. She wanted to stay outside and play with it in the snow, and was so excited and got ready right away. But after only a couple of minutes she ran upstairs and jumped right next to me. I was quite irritated about it at first, but then she told me how she got so scared because she thought she had seen a ghost. Well, she thought the angel she saw was a ghost, because she told me it looked so different from the angels she usually sees: this angel had multi-coloured hair and something that was red and white on its forehead, and many brown spots on its face (moles?) and it looked like a boy angel.

These experiences have really enriched the relationship between my daughter and me, and I love that she now feels she can tell me all about her experiences. However, my husband is really sceptical and does not want to discuss angels at all. I know my daughter really sees angels, I don't doubt it at all, she would never ever make up anything like that. You can tell when children speak the truth.

Listening to our children (and sometimes asking the right question) is something we can all improve on for sure! And, as Jenni discovered, you never know what your children keep from you!

Here is Vicky's experience.

Angels in the Garden

I had a fairly strict upbringing. I was one of six children, so I am happy that my mother had to keep discipline in her large brood. Bedtimes were fairly firm, and I remember one day when my sister and I were fast asleep as usual, I awoke to the sound of tapping on the window. It was brave of me to even get out of bed to investigate the source of the tapping, but a peek out of the bedroom window showed nothing.

Even though wandering around in the night was not permitted, curiosity had me wandering out of the bedroom and into my brothers' room. The boys were both asleep but the tapping could now clearly be heard coming from their window. When I looked outside I couldn't have been more shocked: I counted seven angels in the back garden and they were telling me that I was very special. I remember being confused that I could hear what they were saying even though they were outside the house.

I rushed into my parents' room and my mum was intrigued enough to follow me into the boys' room. The angels were still in the garden. They were large and had wings and I described this to my mother, but disappointingly she could see nothing and told me I must be dreaming. I remember crying and telling my mother that they were waving. One of the angels communicated that they would be watching over me, and he explained that my mother could not see them.

Suddenly the room filled with the scent of flowers. It was so strong that even Mum could smell it. She asked me if I had been spraying her perfume (I hadn't)! At least I felt half-vindicated!

Don't you love that children can see angels? I do! Here is another story. This one was sent by Marrianne.

Paris's Guardian Angel

After trying so hard for a baby for 12 years, I became pregnant naturally with my little girl. I called her Paris.

Things had been hard for several years because I had lost my twin boys at birth. I had been to have psychic readings and was always told that one day I would give birth to a baby girl.

One day when Paris was toddling, she wandered a bit far from me in a car park. A car came from nowhere and skidded right up to her. I was in complete shock and unable to move, but she just she stopped dead as if she had been shouted at. It was a crazy moment and I have never been able to work out why Paris stopped so suddenly. It certainly saved her life, as the car skidded right up to her side ... but missed her. God kept her safe for me that day and he must have sent Paris an angel.

Now Paris is seven years old and she hears things and knows things that others don't. One day she told me a mirror was going to fall off a wall – and she was right. Another day Paris told me that my mobile phone was going to blow while it was on charge. I told her it was a silly thing to say, but just as she said it did blow! She has an intuition about things like when a light bulb will go, too.

As you will see later on, a lot of our new children have a knowing or an ability with electrical items. It's very intriguing!

Many people believe that we come to Earth for our souls to learn and grow. They believe that we plan certain experiences and 'lessons' into our lives before we are born. Even if this were the case (and to be honest it does make a lot of sense to me), it seems that in this next instance it was time for the 'lesson' to STOP. I wonder what happened here? This woman has asked to remain anonymous, and I have purposely left this story ambiguous for the sake of my younger readers.

Safe from Harm

I was just ten years old and waiting on the edge of my bed as always. I was staring out the window wishing I had wings so I could just fly away. I waited for those familiar footsteps coming up the stairs. The door opened and there he was. 'Games' he called them; one after the other we used to play for years and years. I used to feel special because I was allowed to stay up late, but I always ended up crying.

This night started out as normal, then I decided to make a change. I shut my eyes. Usually he would tell me to keep them open. I took myself to a place where I had been before, where everything smiled and everyone danced, such a magical place to be. I felt safe in my special place and there were no pain and no sadness.

All of a sudden there was the biggest, brightest white light I had ever seen. It completely filled the room. I sat up, looking around, feeling so warm as if someone loving was holding me tight. I wasn't scared. In fact, I had never felt so safe and so loved, and even now I can remember the smile that was on my face.

The man hurting me seemed startled by the visitor too. He jumped up from my bed, got dressed and ran out of my room. This was the last time he ever visited me, and for the first time in years I slept through the night and didn't wet the bed.

Now, years later, I believe my protector was my guardian angel. She gave me wings that night. She saved me and I still feel her by my side even now.

Lights and Orbs

Angels in the House

I have a five-year-old little girl called Katie. She is very special and I've always known there was 'something' about her. About eight months ago I was sitting on the floor folding clothes, when out of nowhere Katie said, 'Mom, there are two angels by that chair.' I was stunned and I asked her what they looked like. She explained to me that they were white and had wings.

Since that day she lets me know when they are around. She says they do not talk to her but she is never afraid of them. She says sometimes they are blue and other times grey, pink or purple. She says some are very little and some much bigger.

Katy does have other abilities too. She also seems to know when Daddy is coming home before he is even on our street. Then last year for my birthday my husband bought me a digital camera and we picked up quite a few orbs on the images. When I pointed this out to Katie in some pictures she said, 'No, Mom, those are not orbs, those are angels!'

Other readers have told me that their children say these 'orbs' (or balls of light) which appear on photographs are angels. I believe they can be many things including dust, insects, water vapour and even spirit energy. It's great to think that some orbs might also be angels.

Here is Jan's story:

Angel Orbs?

The very first time that my grandson ever told me about the things he could see, he was around four years old. We were both in a store with just the clerk and as we were leaving the store my grandson asked me if I saw the man. I asked him, 'What man?' He said the man behind the counter. It was a woman clerk, so when I asked him again, 'What man?' he said, 'The one I could see through.'

I explained to him it could have been someone the woman was close to who had passed over, and I told him I could not see him. I explained that God had given him a very special gift and that seemed to ease his mind.

As he is getting older he now knows all the kids don't believe as we do. He is seven years old and the only thing that has scared him was seeing orbs. I told him they are angels watching over him and he felt comfortable with this explanation.

Clearly Jan's grandson was able to see the orbs without a camera lens, although it concerns me when children are frightened by these things. I always wonder if they are picking up stuff that we are not. In most cases it is fear of the unknown rather than a 'logical' fear about what they are experiencing.

Sherri's daughter sees a similar phenomenon. She told me:

> When my daughter sees lights she says they're her angels. She's five and a half now and has been seeing them since she was a toddler. I'm not sure if she can differentiate between a spirit guide, angel and ghost. She told me that they come in different colours and that some of the colours are bad. She tells the bad ones to go away.

Josette told me,

> There are black dots that people get from damage to the retina. Floats or black dots happen when you take a picture looking into the sun, use tanning beds and or strain the eyes under bright lights (like those used in the entertainment field). You get scarring to the retina.
>
> I am constantly under bright lights one way or the other due to my work and through years of working side-stage at rock concerts as a personal assistant, so I had no idea when the doctor told me that just a snapshot with a camera can cause retinal scarring ... then you see black dots.
>
> Maybe not all of the time ... like I don't see them all of the time. Orbs are so different. It's even a different movement. We caught two on film the other night and sent the pictures off to the paranormal society. They called back wanting to stay the night in our house. We

said no! We will keep our ghosties to ourselves right now; we just wanted validation of the photo!

Sue's granddaughter saw floating lights. Here is her story.

Blue Floating Lights

India (my granddaughter) has seen two lights in my house, about two months apart. The first one she saw down by my front door, only a small one but she ran to the front door only to be disappointed that it had vanished.

The second was in my kitchen, only at first I didn't think it was a light she saw. She suddenly said, 'What's that, Nan?' She ran into the kitchen and I asked her, 'What did you see? Was it as big as you or me?' (I thought she'd seen a person.) She said, 'No, it was small and floated across the kitchen to the kitchen door, and it was dark blue.' The look on her face told me it had scared her. I didn't want her to be scared of what she sees, so I smiled and said, 'India, you are so lucky to see that, not many people can see lights like you and me ... you are such a lucky girl.' A big grin appeared on her face! Phew! I took the fear away and now she looks forward to seeing lights in my house and has promised she will tell me when she sees another one.

Didn't Sue handle this so well? Children are often frightened of their paranormal experiences because of the reaction of those around them. The more down-to-earth and casual we can be about it, the better. Sue managed to make India feel special, which was even better! Sometimes children see spirits which seem to appear in different colours too. One woman told me, 'I have been working with my grandson to help him understand his own spirit visions. One spirit he sees a lot is called "captain", and apparently the "captain" glows green!'

Mary says, 'My grandson told me the "bad" spirits glow red and the good ones glow green. There are some he sees that don't glow but their faces are blurry …'

Kim has plenty of experience with this phenomenon.

Grandmother Angel Dots?

My son was in my bedroom this week at night-time. He told me very matter-of-factly, 'There are no dots in this room, Mom.'

My son sees dots in his and his siblings' room. I have a major reason to believe my grandmother watches over the children during the night. When she passed, the whole first year after her death I could smell food cooking in my child's room (back when there was only my toddler daughter).

Once when my daughter and I slept in a different home completely alone, I walked into her room in the middle of the night and it smelled exactly the same as her room at our former home. The smell of food cooking was so strong my husband could smell it, too … it was thick in the air. The smell was present from the time she fell asleep until the time she woke up (6 a.m.-ish?). As soon as she sat up and got out of bed, the smell would magically disintegrate! It manifested every single day for the entire year from the time my grandma passed.

Tanya's daughter had a constant companion who seemed to help her through some of her more difficult childhood experiences.

Invisible Friend?

When my daughter Caitlin was about three years old she started talking to an invisible friend whom she called Bubbles. My little girl would sit and talk to Bubbles for hours and play games whilst saying, 'Bubbles says she wants to play this …' or 'Bubbles has told me to do that …' Sometimes she'd say, 'Don't sit there, you're sitting on Bubbles,' or 'Don't forget to fasten Bubbles' seat belt.'

I asked my daughter to describe what her little friend looked like. She was a young child with blonde hair, similar to my daughter, and when I asked her why I couldn't see her, she said Bubbles was shy! I went along with it all, and to be honest I thought she'd grow out of it. Then one day my partner (at the time) went to see a medium and came back shocked. The medium knew my daughter Caitlin had a spirit guide who had come to help her and to give her confidence (Caitlin had been bullied by other children). I was so shocked that this medium, whom we didn't know, had been able to pick up this information, especially since she lived so far away from us. From then on I began to look at Bubbles in a different light. I was glad this spirit child had come to help my daughter, and was amazed by the fact my daughter Caitlin could see her and was not afraid.

Actually I did see Bubbles once. I was hanging out the washing and I saw her out of the corner of my eye. It was a strange experience, because when you see these things you always doubt yourself.

Claire kindly wrote to tell me about her son Jamie.

Spirit Boy

Jamie is just four and he talks to spirits a lot. Some people say it could be because he is an only child and as I am a single parent studying as well, he does get lonely.

He knows things. He tells me names of people who were family members, and talks to spirit children a lot. One day when he was just three he was playing in the corner with his cars when he waved goodbye to the wall. When I asked him about this he told me he was playing with a little boy and he could not go with this little boy because the boy had been 'deaded' by a green car.

He talks to an aunt of mine who I know is around us both a lot. But my little boy is an angel himself, and to know there are people looking after him as well as me gives me hope when I need it. I think they stay with him to help him through the bad time he has had. I thank them all for helping him.

Children can be so matter-of-fact about their experiences. Very young children often don't even query what is happening to them because they are too young to know that everyone can't see what they see. Louise's daughter was very young when she started to see her own 'visitors'.

The Man

I have just read your book, *An Angel by My Side,* and I do believe in the afterlife.

My daughter Cara was born in 1998 and when she was three months old she would look into the air and follow something with her eyes and give a little gurgle.

We moved house when she was a year old and I started to notice the same phenomenon happening again with her. The difference this time was that she would point and laugh.

At one time she was playing and my sister was sat on a chair near the door. Cara suddenly jumped on my sister's knee and said that the 'man' had scared her coming down the stairs! My surprised sister just looked at me.

Often when she went to bed at night I could hear her talking to someone. I like to think it is my spirit family because I know that children can often do this.

When she reached the age of four she told me about an 'invisible' friend she had, called Alicia. Cara went into great detail describing her friend, and told me that Alicia is the same age as her but with white hair and blue eyes. Apparently she has wings too and sleeps on the top bunk bed.

Of course children do have an active imagination, but most children will be able to tell you if their friend is 'make believe' or 'real' ... to them at least. I think you'll agree that these stories make you think!

The stories in the next chapter will challenge you even more ... and may even frighten you a little. My conclusions are that there is nothing to be afraid of, but you might want to read this chapter during daylight hours ... or leave it altogether ... for now at least! Not everything is as it seems!

CHAPTER 5

Mysterious Visitors

Of course it is possible that UFOs really do contain
aliens as many people believe, and the government is
hushing it up.

Professor Stephen Hawking on C Span Television.

The US Air Force assures me that UFOs pose no threat
to national security ...

President John F Kennedy

'You're not my real parents, my real parents are in space,
and I come from somewhere out there ...' four-year-
old Mike Oram said matter-of-factly to his stunned parents.

What he said next was so profound, and he used
such mature language, that his mother has never forgotten either the phrase or the moment Mike told her.
'Something of incredible importance is going to happen
on this Earth, not in your lifetime but in mine. It is to
do with global consciousness and that is why I am here

at this time, to experience this change ...' said the young boy. No wonder his mother never forgot!

Where do these ideas come from? Is it something remembered from a TV programme or are our children repeating overheard adult conversation? Can it really be possible that Mike's spirit has brought special memories with him into this lifetime? Honestly? This really is the most logical explanation to me ... but then I have the benefit of having read so many similar case histories! I am convinced that many of our psychic children are highly advanced souls with a mission here on Earth.

Would this phrase from a small child explain why more and more people (children in particular) are experiencing such frequent paranormal and psychic phenomena at this moment in time? I really believe the consciousness of each and every one of us is changing, ready for this exciting time in our human history. More people than ever are having 'psychic experiences' – or occasional moments of intuition and sixth-sense abilities. Psychic children are the rule rather than the exception, according to my research.

The *New York Times* best-selling author Gary Zukav, in his book, *Soul Stories*, says '... everyone is becoming multisensory ...' meaning that we are all increasingly able to use abilities outside our 'traditional' five senses. Natural intuition in many human beings is growing stronger, and lots of people are increasingly using what they call their 'gut instincts', or inner feelings, to guide them.

If my own postbag is anything to go by, many children are being born with these extra abilities already in place. They are able to pick up a wider range of information (like cats and dogs do naturally) which is outside our 'normal' (or traditional), limited human senses. And this includes the ability to communicate with advanced beings who appear to sit outside this 'normal' range of senses. There have always been 'psychic' adults, but now the numbers are growing and, as you can see, some of these abilities are astounding (if not a little scary!). What is going on?

Many of these children behave in unusual ways. Their understanding and view of the world are different from ours. Let's look at some of the evidence.

Teresa is from the US. Here is her story.

Child from Another Place?

My friend's daughter has been seeing ghosts and communicating with them for a long time now. She is 11 years old. My friend once woke up to the smell of breakfast being cooked by her daughter when she was just six years old. She had made a complete breakfast of bacon, eggs and toast and had set the table for six people (there are only three in the family). Her mom asked her what she was doing and she told her that her friends were hungry and had explained to her what to cook and how to do it. Freaky, huh?

My friend lives across the street from my in-laws, and my in-laws have a Doberman Pincher. Every time this child comes to the fence the dog's hair stands on end and it growls. This dog never exhibits this behaviour to any other child. It's as if the dog is picking up something it is frightened of or perhaps doesn't understand. My own little dog has never bitten anyone and is eight years old, but whilst the kids were playing in the basement my dog actually snapped at this girl. Never before have I seen my dog act in such a scared way.

The family live on five acres of land, and when they go mushroom hunting this little girl always sees a lot of 'people' in the wooded area. She has pointed them out to her parents and of course they don't see anything at all.

She can be unpredictable too. She was once found riding her bike to the local lake (which is three miles away) at three a.m.! Now her mom sleeps with her and has a lock on the bedroom door so that she can't get out.

She's had this child in and out of hospitals and she has had to be put on medication just to get her to sleep all night long.

This young girl does sound unusual. Animals are often aware of the differences and pick them out right away. There is a growing number of people who believe that many advanced souls are being born into human bodies at this time. As we've discussed already, these souls are here to help us. Often when they are born they have no memory of this mission (although sometimes I've discovered that the children have always known why they were born). Adults around them may be aware of extraordinary behaviour which alerts them to this possibility, and even though the facts seem clear they still ask me, 'Is this right? Can this be real?' I like to put them in touch with other parents so they can discuss it among themselves. There's nothing more helpful than chatting to someone in the same situation!

Some children are regularly visited by advanced spirits (from our dimension, other dimensions and other worlds) who teach them about their future roles on Earth. Sounds bizarre? I'm with you on that one, but read on!

One woman from the US wrote to tell me about her son.

Answer to the Mystery of Life?

When my son was almost four, we were sitting at the table cutting, pasting and coloring. He cut out a long strip of yellow paper with a bump in the middle. Inside the bump he made two circles. He told me one was the life of heaven and the other was the life of the Earth. Then he cut a green circle, glued it to the bottom of the strip, and told me that it was the Earth. Then he cut out an 'e' and glued it to the top of the strip. He told me it was the 'e' for 'everything'. Then he had me cut out a heart and pasted the outline of the heart onto the 'e'. He told me it was his love on top of the 'e' for everything.

Then he taped his creation on our living-room wall and told me I needed to leave it there for one year. I have a picture of it and am saving it in his baby book for when he is older.

A few nights ago, he told me that he was going to go to heaven early. He needs to 'take care of things'. This statement (as with others in the past) scared me, but I tried not to let him see that. He wants to be president when he grows up. He says he will stop all of the wars and everyone will love and take care of everyone else. It's noble and maybe a normal dream, but he believes he will do it.

These big plans and enlightened ideas are common amongst these 'new children'. They often seem wiser than any adult!

Mum Kerry told me about her daughter Kim.

Changing the World

Kim is now 11 and we have always known that there was something different about her. She has always been very spiritual and has a lovely peace about her. All her school teachers have commented on it.

About a year ago a strange woman approached me and told me that my grandfather was my spirit guide and that he wanted me to visit a medium. This intrigued me, so a few weeks later I found a medium.

During my visit she told me that my eldest daughter was psychic, clairaudient (which translates as 'hear-spirit'). I was a little shocked, but then it made some sense.

For a long time we had been experiencing ghosts in our home. I was OK with it but my husband was freaked out. I told the medium that I knew Kim could see energy fields around people and that she would often cry at night when she would hear lots of voices in her room, so many that she could not make out what any of them were saying.

The medium suggested that Kim should call her angels and command all the voices to stop, but invite one to step forward and give their name. She did this, and we were blown away by the outcome. The first spirit she spoke to was her Polish grandmother, who told her that she had been waiting a long time to communicate with her and basically told her that she had a great purpose on Earth and that she would be there to help her. She told her that there would be signposts along the way and ' ... things will become clearer'. She actually told Kim, 'You are here to change the world!'

She still comes back to her from time to time. Since then, Kim has had many conversations with spirits. She can see, hear and sense them and her abilities grow all the time.

Thousands upon thousands of people (children and adults) around the world are having contact with beings from other planets and realms. Surely not every one of them is crazy?

Young children – and adults – of all ages, races and intelligence have seen and experienced 'off-world vehicles,' unidentified flying objects (UFOs) and beings from other places and dimensions (more commonly called 'aliens' or extraterrestrials/ETs). Many adults have had experiences their whole lives, starting from when they were very young indeed. Belief in these visitors is one which is held by some esteemed company.

On June 27, 1982, then-US president Ronald Reagan watched a preview of the classic movie *ET: The Extraterrestrial*. The film focuses on a young 'off-world' being who becomes stuck on Earth. The young alien struggles to return home, but is aided by some friendly Earth children. All the while he is on the planet he is chased by government agencies.

Sitting with the president whilst he watched the film was his wife Nancy and the movie's director, Steven Spielberg, as well as several other invited guests. At the end of the film, President Reagan leaned over to Spielberg and stated, 'You know, I bet there aren't six people in this room who know just how true this really is.' Clearly President Reagan knew a lot more than he was letting on!

President Reagan wasn't the only US president to have made such comments about our visitors from other planets. During his presidential campaign, Jimmy Carter stated, 'If I become president, I'll make every piece of information this country has about UFO sightings available to the public and scientists. I am convinced that UFOs exist because I have seen one.' (He didn't make all the information available ... so either he never got to find out – even the president isn't told everything – or there wasn't anything to find out.)

I find it hard to believe that there is no truth whatsoever to the many, many millions of UFO sightings around the world! Of course the government will deny it – would you admit that there were foreign vessels in our skies that you could do nothing about? It doesn't say much for national security, does it? 'Well … erm, yes, there are craft which are flown by beings from out in space but we … erm … don't know who they are … and erm … don't know if they are a threat or not …' YES, you can see the predicament!

I can assure you that flying saucers, given that they exist, are not constructed by any power on Earth.

President Harry S. Truman, 1950

There are estimated to be a hundred billion stars in the Milky Way alone. How many more galaxies are there out there, and how many more millions of stars, planets and alien worlds do we know nothing about? Is it likely that life exists that we can't even see? Of course there is life out there! Not only is there life out there, but there is life 'in here'.

There always has been other life interacting with our own, and there always will be. There is so much we don't understand about how our world works. Remember when we believed that if you set sail in a ship you would eventually fall off the edge of the Earth? Of course we

know today that isn't what happens. We didn't understand the simple fact of gravity and that the Earth is
round.

Of course there are many more universal rules that
we don't understand and can't even begin to bring into
our belief system. I always used to laugh at scientists
who suggested that life would need sunlight, oxygen,
etc., etc. How do we know that? We haven't even discovered every living creature on our own lands and in the
deepest part of our own seas. Seriously. We don't have a
clue, do we? You only have to look at the diversity of life
on our own small planet to know that we haven't even
begun to scratch the surface. As they say in the old *Star
Trek* series, 'It's life, Jim … but not as we know it.' (I
couldn't have put it better myself.)

With this in mind, I take the stories of alien encounters very seriously indeed. Let's go back to Mike Oram's
intriguing story.

As a young boy, Mike (whom we talked about at the
beginning of the chapter) began having visits from a being
he called his 'space brother', a being from another realm.
At first his visitor appeared to him in disguise. I asked Mike
to share more of his fascinating experiences with me.

Encounters with the Space Brother

Mike was nearing seven years of age when he awoke in
the middle of the night. Mike was aware of a presence in

his room, someone who seemed to be wearing a space-suit. He clearly remembers the silver colour was shimmering in the darkness; it reminded him of tin foil. Next he heard the being's voice speaking inside his head. The spaceman was communicating with him and gave his name as 'Tellos', explaining that he lived in the stars but was never far away. He then held his hand up in a peace gesture before he disappeared. But this was just the start of a long friendship.

Eventually Mike got back to sleep and in the morning he found a card on his bed. He was excited when he picked it up and saw that the image on the front of the card showed the same spaceman who had appeared the night before. On the back of the card was a map of a solar system and it had a list of the planets that Tellos had visited, including the Earth. Mike ran and showed the card to his mother and told her what had happened the night before. She did not quite know what to make of it, but as she had already had many weird conversations with her son she didn't dismiss it entirely!

This card seemed to provide the 'proof' that many people ask for with these types of encounters. Mike remembers holding the card every single day. He would stare at the face and look at the star system on the reverse and the journeys the spaceman had made, and try to imagine what it would be like to go to other star systems and planets.

He told me, 'When I held the card in my hand, I felt a strong energy of love and connection; a bond, a bond that existed through time and space.' Mike believes the visits (both his and others') are partly to help us raise our consciousness so that we know for sure that 'reality' is far greater than we have been taught.

Mike's visitors have contacted him throughout his life, and these visits are still happening now. Sometimes the visits are more frequent and at other times the visits are spaced apart. He usually gets some sort of feeling that a visit is approaching, so they don't catch him out like they once did.

At one point Mike found a special green stone after a visit, which he feels was also left by his 'space brother'. He feels that the items were not given to him for any particular reason or purpose, but says that when he held the items he could feel a connection to his off-world friends almost as if the items had been impregnated with their energy. The card in particular held a presence of Tellos, and Mike felt that the green stone connected him to the universe itself.

Mike says,

I had it for two years, until one day it mysteriously disappeared. I kept the green stone for just over a year until my mother threw it away, because of 'paranormal phenomena' that she associated with the stone. I miss them even to this day.

Like many others, Mike understands that these things are happening for a very good reason. He is one of many thousands around the world who are now awakening to this higher divine purpose. He says, 'I believe that we are on the cusp of an evolutionary shift in consciousness; necessary if we are ever to be ready to take our part in the universal community.'

Mike's story is fascinating and he has written a book about his experiences. You can read about his encounters in his excellent book, *Does It Rain in Other Dimensions?*

At no time when the astronauts were in space were they alone: there was a constant surveillance by UFOs.

NASA's Scott Carpenter

Visiting to Help Us?

Many people wrote to tell me about their own children's unusual understanding of alien encounters, or shared their own children's experiences. Kim told me:

Here to Help Us?

I am the last person I ever thought would want to talk about this subject. My son is five. About two weeks ago he walked over to me very matter-of-factly and told me that aliens live in Massachusetts. Well, possibly he said that state because he knows his uncle is moving there now.

I asked my son about it, and said casually, 'Have you ever seen an alien?' I thought he would start to tell me about something frightening he might have seen on the television, but he didn't. He told me, 'Yes.' When I asked what they're like, he replied, 'They're nice and they're here to help us.'

I went home and got out one of my old Sylvia Brown books. I know she's talked about aliens before and believes in them. I've always purposely skipped those sections of her books because I felt I was not ready to be scared by that kind of information. I just knew it wasn't going to be pretty and I wouldn't be able to sleep nights any more. Well, I opened to the section on aliens and read the whole thing. Nothing scary at all! As a matter of fact, her theme was the same as my son's. They come here to help us. She says they don't want to take over our planet or anything like that because we've already ruined it. But they like to watch us and help us if they can.

Visiting to Help Them?

Sadly, although most encounters are positive, occasionally they are not. Stefan has clear memories of being taken away from the house during the night when he was a child. His feelings towards these experiences are not terribly pleasant and frighten him still to this day. I have discovered that the more information children are given by their off-world visitors, the less frightened they become.

Taken

In my middle thirties I started having serious nightmares relating to my childhood experiences. I became paranoid about the dark and couldn't sleep at night without having the light on. I have memory flashbacks relating to when I was five years old. I remember one night going into my parents' room and shouting at my parents to remove the strange people from my bedroom.

At the time we lived in Selly Oak in Birmingham in the UK. I have photograph of my family standing on the front lawn of our house at the time. When I look at the image now it reminds me of a night when my brother and I were standing in that exact spot late one night. I was five and my brother was seven. I remember a very bright light surrounding us both and nothing could be seen through it. I have no conscious memory of what happened next.

I remember when I was 11 years old waking up to another bright light. The light was intense and formed a beam. I felt myself lifted up into the light, and then the next memory I have is of lying on a shiny metal table with strange beings looking down at me.

There were two different types of beings. The tall skinny ones reminded me of the cartoon character the Pink Panther (without the tail). They had big black eyes and seemed to float around. The shorter beings were grey and wrinkly with a strong odour. They seemed to be examining me and they understood and communicated with me using my thoughts.

On another day I had been mowing the lawn and spotted a bright light in the sky. My parents witnessed it too, and the sighting was reported in the local newspaper.

Other younger members of my family had similar experiences. One was also five when she remembers being woken in the night. A bright light filled the room and she too saw strange 'people' moving around the house.

My granddad had a recollection of seeing a bright light in the forest when he was a young man in Poland. He went to investigate it and suddenly found himself walking in the opposite direction. When he looked at his watch, two hours had gone by!

Stefan told me that the beings he encountered do not travel from far distant regions of our galaxy. He says they travel between dimensions, and this is how they manipulate matter using thought. He believes that the aliens that track him and his family (often families over many generations) are doing so for their own means. He believes they may be running precise long-term experiments. You can reach Stefan at www.paranormalawakening.com.

Stefan's story stirred something inside me. Stefan and I are a similar age. I too lived in Birmingham, UK as a child, and I too used to wake up and see something half-transparent in my room at night!

This next woman is well aware of communication down through the generations of families. I'll let her tell her story in her own words.

The UFO People

My name is Bonnie Jean Hamilton, and I am a lifelong friend of the star people. I have known them since I was a young child, and my children also know them. Now I help other abductees and contactees deal with their experiences.

When I was a baby, I took in every detail of my life with curiosity and wonder, whether I was awake or asleep. I innately knew that everything was alive with energy; nobody told me this – in fact, I realized that most of the people in my life did not understand this concept. It was my own.

When my loving parents set me down in my crib to rest, I continued to observe my environment and learn. When the lights went out and I was alone in the darkness, I desired to take in more data; I was intrigued by all aspects of life and I never wanted to miss a thing. As a young child I had no fear of the darkness, only a curious amazement.

Though my eyes were temporarily blinded, moving from light to dark, I did not let that deter me; I knew there was more to see even when the forces of light were extinguished. I stared into the blackness, searching for any kind of movement that might catch my eye – and I found it. Whether these first movements were created by small particles of light, reflections in my eyes, my inner mind or detections of another reality, it made no difference; there was life. I watched with wonder and awe as colored shapes took form wherever my eyes could focus and hold that attention still.

Each and every night, when the lights went out I stared into the darkness of my room, looking for something to focus on. Slowly, the images began to appear: candy, toys, animals, smiling faces. Many times, these images were fleeting glimpses of passing objects and people, as though I were observing their actions in another life from afar. I was fascinated and always kept my eyes wide open to see what came next. The people I saw sometimes looked back at me and moved their lips, as if they were speaking to me, but I could not hear what they were saying.

Then, one night when I was four years old, two figures appeared in my peripheral vision while I was watching the pictures in the dark. I sat up in my bed, turned to focus on them and watched as these two small people with large, bulbous heads walked toward the foot of my bed. I focused my full attention on them, bringing them into clear focus. What I saw were two very thin stick people with large round heads, holding hands, slowly and methodically moving closer and closer toward me. Their profiles were black, so no specific features were visible to my eyes. I find this interesting, considering I was already in complete darkness, so no illumination was present at all – why were their faces concealed when other aspects were clear to me? Perhaps it was their choice not to fully reveal themselves, or perhaps it was my own mind not wanting to recall all the details.

It was the first time I had been able to bring any of the people in these images into vivid attention, and the reality of it frightened me. I screamed aloud and my mother quickly entered the room. As she did, the two figures vanished. After this encounter with the beings whom I believe to be 'star people', I became fearful of the dark to a certain extent. I needed comfort and reassurance that everything was OK when I went to sleep. In particular, I was afraid of two knots on the wooden door of the bedroom – I explained to my parents that the spots looked like big eyes. For a while, I needed a night light to help me sleep. My parents sat with me every night, read stories to me and sang to me. They were loving and as understanding as they could be, but they did not know what was happening.

By the time I was seven years old I had faced my fear and I was no longer afraid of the dark. My next conscious encounter with the star people occurred once again as I lay in my bed watching images float around my bedroom. This time, my eyes focused on the dolls sitting on a shelf across the room. They were the toys I played with every day, so they were, by nature, non-threatening. When the first doll winked her eye and stood up, I was surprised, but I stayed calm and kept my eyes on her. Another doll joined her in a voiceless conversation (I could see their lips moving, but could not hear the sound of their voices). They held hands, stepped off the shelf, and grew in size to about four foot high as they reached the floor.

I was looking at two small star people standing across the room from me. Their features were clear to me and their heads were less bulbous and disproportionate than the first encounter when I was four. They walked toward my bed as I calmly watched them release hands, one stopping near the foot of the bed and one continuing to the head of the bed, just to the upper left of my head. I felt completely at ease, already familiar with the routine; I threw back the blankets, kicked my feet over the side as I sat up, jumped off the bed and took the open hand of the star person standing to my left. The other star person stepped over to join us as we held hands and walked out of the bedroom, past my sleeping parents, through the kitchen and living room, and out the front door into the night.

This is my conscious memory – what happened in between four and seven years of age remains hidden in my mind. Obviously, whatever happened, I was able to overcome my fear of these people and learn to be comfortable with their presence and with holding their hands and walking side by side with them. When I spoke to my parents about these events, they told me I was dreaming and that dreams were not real, so I should not worry about what happened in dreams. I knew in my heart that my parents were mistaken; they just did not have the same experiences I did. I was always open-minded, and no matter what happened I kept my eyes open and tried my best to stay alert even if I felt tired or frightened.

The next life-changing encounter with the star people happened when I was 11 years old. One evening as I was drifting off to sleep, I saw a bright light streak past the bedroom window. I jumped up and ran to see what it could have been. What I saw made my mouth drop and my eyes pop wide open – a UFO landing in the parking lot next door. I excitedly ran through the house and out the door to the side yard. The occupants of the craft were exiting one by one and walking toward me. There were five of them, tall and thin with white skin and normal-sized heads. We stood around the picnic table in my yard and ate a snack they had brought with them. I stared in awe and watched every move, completely fascinated by these friendly star people. They seemed to be equally fascinated by me, but not unfamiliar, as they called me by name and smiled as they spoke. 'We will come back to see you again,' they said, and I woke in my bed.

How I was waking a second time, I did not understand; nonetheless, I woke my three cousins (who were staying with me at the time) and explained the whole thing. Aliens had landed! We spent the day searching for UFO marks in the parking lot and any possible clues of UFO activity. We didn't find much of anything except for a few oil blotches left by parked cars. I was a bit disappointed, but I watched the night sky for weeks afterward.

As I got older, my interests and attention turned to schoolwork, marching band, majorettes, track team, talent shows, playing the guitar, and boys. I excelled in my studies and skipped 11th grade to graduate from high school a year early. Not long afterward, I married my first husband and gave birth to my first daughter. As my life began to change and I began to settle down a bit, my encounters with the star people became a startling reality I was forced to face – not only were the star people visiting me, I was quite aware they were visiting my young daughter as well.

During many of my experiences with the star people, my daughter was right there with me. These events occurred from about the time she was three years old until she was seven. When we were together in the presence of star people, everything was fine; we were not mistreated in any way, and we were both fairly comfortable with these other-world people. However, she also went away with them on her own (without me), which was difficult for me to deal with because I was so concerned for her wellbeing. I would usually go searching for her and, a couple times, I even had the assistance of other star people bringing her back home when I was overly anxious for her safe return. Of course, the star people completely understood my feelings, but they were not accustomed to parents coming to pick up their kids from the spaceship!

When she was three or four years old, my daughter began to speak openly about 'Tee' and his spaceship in the sky. She explained that she would visit Tee and all the little children who lived in his house with him.

His 'house above the road' had pretty lights and lots of round windows, and she always enjoyed playing with the other children. Probably because I was so 'understanding' about the subject, she was very comfortable speaking to me and everyone else in the family about it.

One night, the whole family had an experience which we recounted in the morning when we woke. At that time, I had remarried and given birth to another daughter, so there were four of us. During my experience that night, my husband and I were standing outside the house watching a group of lights zigzag around the sky. We wondered if they would come closer and perhaps pay us a visit, but we got tired of waiting and went back inside to go to sleep. On our way to the bedroom, I peeked in at my oldest daughter. She sat up in her bed and looked at me in a dazed fashion, and I immediately knew she had been with the star people.

Suddenly, a bright light shone down onto her bed from the ceiling. She happily jumped up into the light, with my husband following her. I knew they were going on board the spaceship, and I was about to join them when my youngest daughter (then two years old) yelled out, 'Mommy!' which physically woke me. I jumped out of bed and ran to her side. She asked me, 'Mommy, where are you going?' I told her that I wouldn't go anywhere, and that seemed to comfort her. I went back to sleep and watched the lights of the spaceship through the walls and ceiling of our house, but I did not go out.

In the morning as we shared details of the encounter, my husband said he recalled seeing lights inside the house. My oldest daughter (then seven years old) said that the star people came down in their spaceship and landed in the yard. One of them got out and walked around. He was contemplating whether or not to bring the whole family on the ship. My youngest daughter was explaining to us that she saw different colored lights in the road, shining down over the street, when my older daughter burst in, 'Yeah, the spaceship was there.'

From what other contactees have reported, and from my own experience, it seems that this connection with the star people runs through family lines. If you are an abductee or contactee, it is likely someone else in your family is, too. Children who are afraid of the dark need to be comforted and loved, and children who experience intense and vivid dreams should be listened to and given the attention they deserve. Sometimes dreams are more than just the mind's way of going through daily events – dreams can be the gateway to other worlds in which real, valid events are taking place. And when children come into this world and are just learning what the rules of this reality are, they are very open to metaphysical experience, so please pay attention to them!

I found Bonnie Jean Hamilton to be a lovely, very sane and normal person indeed. She does have a website and if you want to contact her about her experiences you can reach her at www.alienabductionhelp.com.

The Expert Opinion

To get a little perspective on the phenomenon of alien visitors, I decided to interview an expert in the field. I asked Nick Pope (who used to investigate UFOs for the British government) his opinion. Nick is also an author who has published several books on UFOs and the abduction phenomenon. He hasn't had any paranormal experiences himself.

He told me,

> I've looked into around 100 cases of so-called alien abduction. I don't know what these people are experiencing, but I'm convinced that most of them are sincere and genuinely believe they've had these experiences. Most shy away from the media, so we're not dealing with attention-seekers. Similarly, scientific studies have found no evidence of any psychopathology in the abductees.
>
> There are some intriguing parallels between modern alien abduction accounts and folklore concerning encounters with 'the little people', which suggests people have been having these experiences for hundreds of years, if not longer. These experiences tend to start in childhood, but I don't know what the significance, if any, is of this.

I asked Nick if he had any specific thoughts relating to these types of alien child abductions. He said, 'It's a very difficult area, which raises a myriad of ethical issues about the way in which such cases should be investigated, if indeed they should be investigated at all.'

Through my own research I've discovered that most people feel uncomfortable about being identified, but feel that their experiences should be reported and investigated by an official government body. Naturally, investigating cases of off-world encounters with children might possibly cause problems in itself. Some of the adults who have memories of abduction or encounters as children are frightened of uncovering the truth as much as they feel the information needs to be discovered. Of course, once you talk, you open yourself to ridicule and disbelief – it's a hard call!

'Some experiences seem positive and some negative. This may be because the experiences vary, but it may also reflect differences in people's reactions to anomalous experiences,' suggests Nick.

I'm sure he is right. Many accounts that I have read about indicated different versions of the 'memory' of events when looked at under hypnosis. Although hypnosis isn't infallible by any means, many cases show that the 'real' experience, as viewed from this altered state of consciousness, is much less frightening than the suppressed version of events. Under hypnotic trance, many people recall giving permission (of sorts) for these visits to take place. The off-world visitors are often familiar friends whom they have worked with for many years. Other people believe that they are in some way part of these alien races and are themselves here to help humankind.

Nick had some thoughts on this too:

Some people believe that a new generation of human/
alien hybrids are living amongst us and will act as a force
for good for humanity. This idea of 'starkids' has its roots
in the separate but possibly related New Age idea of so-
called Indigo Children.

Only one thing is certain here. Research into this area
is still in its early stages. After many years people are
now starting to take this phenomenon seriously. Whether through fear or ignorance, we are long past the stage
where ridicule is the answer. Just because we don't understand something, are frightened or don't want to listen, it doesn't mean it isn't true!

I have my own thoughts about the phenomenon and
will continue to follow the progress with great interest
… this sounds like a whole other book, so contact me
if this sounds familiar to you! Check out my website for
more information: www.JackyNewcomb.com.

Incidentally, Nick runs a fascinating website too. You
can find him at: www.nickpope.net.

Practical Help

If any of the information in this chapter feels familiar to
you – don't panic! There are reasons why this information
is suppressed! We live a life that we feel we understand.

The human brain often goes haywire when changes take place outside 'normal'.

Moving house, changing jobs, relationships ending and the death of a loved one are just some of the things that can cause great disruption to our mental state. Although most of us show great strength of character during times of stress, there is a very fine line between coping and just 'losing it'.

If there are alien beings contacting us (and there seem to be many thousands of people around the world who believe that there are), then the reason we don't remember everything about these visits is for the protection of our fragile human minds.

I have suspect memories of my own, but that doesn't mean I'm going to discover what they mean ... not yet, anyway (cue future book ... watch this space – and let me know about your own encounters!).

The research I have done into this phenomenon shows that if indeed these visits have taken place, most of them can be revealed to one extent or another through hypnotic regression. During regression, scary memories of alien encounters are often replaced with a great realization that we are meeting up with off-world friends with whom we have agreed to work over our current lifetime in a human body. The fear we recall is mainly due to the bits we have forgotten (or that have been hidden ... maybe for good reason)!

If you choose to decide that the phenomenon is real, then the reality seems to be a safe one in *most* cases.

What you can do to help yourself:

1. Ignore the phenomenon and view it as a strange and unexplainable experience. Carry on with your life as you know it.
2. Be regressed in a hypnotic session (beware, though: once you or your child have opened the lid on these 'memories', whether real or false, you can't put it back!). Be *very sure* that this is something you want to investigate closely at this time.
3. Find groups of others with whom to discuss the phenomenon – the Internet is a great place to start, or your local New Age shop may know others who are interested in chatting with you.
4. Check out seminars and talks around the world relating to alien and UFO phenomena.
5. Learn a little more about the experiences of others through books and so on. Knowledge is power. There are also several UFO magazines published around the world which might be another source of information and contacts.
6. Make notes of the experiences that happen to you or your family (keep records of when, where, how, etc. … everything you can remember).
7. Many believe that children born with these extraordinary 'memories' and abilities have chosen to be born at this time so that they can help humankind, as Nick Pope and others suggest. Feel privileged to be a part of the exciting changes that are taking place

on our world, and if you are a parent of a child with off-world memories, know that you were especially 'chosen' for this role.

See the Further Reading and Resources section at the end of this book for recommendations on books, websites, etc.

Religious Visits/Connections

More and more I am getting stories which relate to religious figures such as Jesus or even God. My favourite reader experiences are those where God gives permission for deceased relatives to pop back and visit the living. This happens more and more … or maybe we are simply more and more aware of it. Loved ones who appear in dreams and visions actually say to their living loved ones, 'God told me I could visit!' Interesting!

Sherri's daughter was aware of a time that existed *before* she was born. Little Kara says that 'God told her it was time' to be born again. Sherri continues:

She told me that it used to be that she was the mommy and I was her little girl. Now we switched [in this lifetime].

I have NEVER spoken to her about reincarnation, yet she tells me that she lived before as my mommy, then died and went to God before He sent her back. I should mention that the only religious exposure she has had is in preschool, where they sang religious songs but did not teach Bible stories.

There is more about this interesting phenomenon in Chapter 8.

Psychic-children expert Lynne Gallagher, author of *Psychic Kids*, is an adept in the new wave of children often described as Indigos and Crystals. She says:

Rainbows are the next lot of kids after the Crystals. They are even more psychically advanced than Crystals and will have the power of bringing peace and understanding to the world. Telepathy, telekinesis and healing are some of the traits they will have. There are a few at the moment, but they will have a total understanding of all things and be able to communicate with God and the ascended masters, like Jesus and Buddha.

Many who once considered this 'psychic mumbo jumbo' are now seeing the truth of these words. It certainly seems hard to deny that many children being born today are very different from previous generations.

Kim told me, 'My daughter told me she heard God talking to her one day (she was three) even though she hadn't been taught about God (yet) in our home or from anyone else.'

This next woman (who has asked to remain anonymous) wrote to tell me about her son's relationship with

Jesus. As she explains, the connection came as a great surprise to her!

Jesus Daddy in the Sky

I stumbled across your website whilst searching for help on the internet. I have a son who is nearly eight years old and I now realize he has been psychic from a very early age.

At 18 months old he would call Jesus 'Daddy'. He would hold this icon above his head and repeat 'Daddy up, up sky.'

We are not really a religious family and I had never spoken to him at such an early age about God or Jesus or heaven.

At the age of three he was obsessed with crystals and collecting precious stones, which he still does. At the age of five he would laugh at his little sister because she was in a 'bubble'. When I questioned him about this, he said we are all in coloured bubbles and he looked puzzled when he asked me, 'Can't you see the bubbles, Mummy?' I explained to him that what he is seeing is called an aura and that he is very special to be able to see them.

Emma's daughter seemed very close to Jesus, and her mum told me about her experiences.

Cuddle Jesus

> Maryellen has always been very sensitive and at one time we couldn't mention Jesus as she would cry because baby Jesus died and was in heaven and she would say she wanted to go to heaven too, and she'd cry because she couldn't go and cuddle Jesus.

That's all we have space for in this book, but I am convinced that advanced beings are visiting and interacting with our children and maybe even that our children are of a superior 'race' or soul group than we are. Call me crazy if you like, but this is such a small selection of the material I have studied and it just feels like the truth to me.

As I have suggested before, if you find this section a little hard to understand or believe, leave it for now and come back to it at a later time. I present all the material in this book not as 'fact' but as something to think about. My beliefs don't have to be the same as your own (though I do believe this is all true) … but do me a favour, will you? Respect the words spoken by good and sincere people, and consider … just think about the fact that we can't possibly know *everything there is to know*. But we DO know that life … as we know it, probably isn't all there is! Right?

Are they really here to help? Many believe that life as we now know it will no longer exist after, or close to the date on or near, 22 December 2012 – the date the ancient Mayan calendar famously ends. Many believe that time and space as we know it are about to change into something new ... and better. The human race is evolving.

Many psychic children say they are here to help us grow spiritually so that we are ready for this important time in history, a time never seen before anywhere in humanity's experience.

'Old souls' are entering children at birth. Their wisdom, knowledge and gentle spirits are changing the very bodies they enter. By doing so, they may also initially struggle to cope with our 'heavy' earthly bodies, so there are a few challenges along the way. It's all worth it as they hold our hands during one of eternity's biggest-ever spiritual ascensions.

Could this 'amazing and unbelievable' statement be true?' Take your time if this information is all new to you. It's mind-blowing ... and time to move on to the next chapter! You don't have to decide right now!

CHAPTER 6

Strange Phenomena

Everything in life is vibration.

Albert Einstein

Paranormal Phenomena

We've already covered a lot of different types of paranormal phenomena in the book. Many parents find the whole thing exhausting and confusing, not least of all because they are faced with the difficulty of not being able to talk about it to others.

Unless you are a part of this strange and wonderful world, it's hard to understand or even believe that any of it is real – but real it is! This woman, who asked to remain anonymous, explained it very well. She told me,

I viewed your website and I was very interested in the information about psychic children. I am experiencing this in a totally different way. I live in a very rural area where this type of gift will not be accepted at all, so

I must keep this confidential within my family. I am a Christian and the things that my child is seeing are scaring me more than him.

... I am very compassionate about my child's fears because my sister has been tormented with this very same 'gift'. I cover my child in prayer to protect him. I feel as though I am battling an unseen world ...

Many of my readers will understand and sympathize!

Death Premonitions or Psychic Link?

Children can sometimes pick up information using their sixth sense in a way that we cannot fully explain. When one of my own daughters was about seven we were all eating breakfast in the kitchen when she randomly asked, 'Who was Daddy's uncle?' She had actually met this man, but only once, and it had been over a year since she had seen him. We had not been talking about him, and this question came out of the blue. We found out later that he had died that very morning.

Clodes, who also has a story in Chapter 6, remembers a similar experience in her own family (I have changed the names as requested here).

Holy God

When my sister was nearly three she went to our mother and said, 'Nana and Aunty Chris are crying because baby

Julie has gone to heaven to be with holy God.' My mother just drove across the city to where they were living, and baby Julie had in fact died about 30 minutes earlier.

The night before our nan died my sister kept having an overwhelming smell of roses. On the day she died I was doing my school exams. Everything was going fine and then at 3.45 p.m. I had a really odd sensation. My body was prickling and I just couldn't write. My mind became blank and all of a sudden I felt this amazing sense of peace and saw a beautiful golden-yellow light as if everywhere was bathed in it. It then occurred to me that my nan had died but that she was OK. I felt the words, '… and she's fine now.' When I got home I was told my nan had died. She had died shortly after 3.45 p.m.

Holly's son was also able to pick up on a family passing, but this time the family were aware of where the information had come from. She told me:

Collected by a Family Angel

I lost my dad back in March. Dad was very close to my oldest son, but before he passed my son told me that his uncle, my brother, whom I lost six years ago, came to him and told him he was here for 'Papaw'. My son even told me what day he was going to pass over.

My son was right, and when I called from the hospital to tell him about it, he already knew.

My son talks about seeing his deceased relatives all the time. He tries to share it with other adults but they just blow him off like he's a kid and doesn't know what he's talking about.

Chatting to Relatives?

Yvette wondered if her child had psychic abilities. Like lots of little ones, Reyna can pick up communication from other 'spaces' or dimensions. She is three and her father has recently suffered an accident which has left him in a coma. Her mother writes:

Daddy's Looking After Me ... For Now

Reyna Cerna was born prematurely. I only carried her in the womb for six months and she weighed just 1lb 3oz. The doctors said she would have lots of problems in life. They said she would be blind and have to spend her life in an oxygen tank. They were wrong. She is now a normal and happy little girl.

Reyna often seems to talk to herself and plays on her own a lot. Sometimes when I am shopping I walk away from the basket for just a second and when I turn back she's pointing up into the air and talking to no one (at least no one I can see). I ask her, 'Who are you talking to, Reyna?' and she will reply, 'I'm not talking to you!' almost as if I am butting in on her conversation.

I haven't told her or her older brother about the whole situation with their father except to tell them that Daddy is very sick in the hospital, and he'll be there for a while. Well, a few days later Reyna said, 'I miss Daddy, but it's OK 'cause he's up there and that's where he's going to watch me for now.' Well, you can guess I was intrigued. I asked her, 'What do you mean "for now"?' She just looked at me and smiled in a knowing sort of a way! She does this a lot.

I know she hasn't heard conversations I've had with other family members, because I tell everyone not to talk about their father in front of the children, no matter what. We always go into another room.

She's really amazing when she's around me, especially when I'm sad or crying. She looks me in the eyes and tells me, 'Mommy, who did it? Who made you cry?' I tell her my problem because she sees me crying already and I feel I should so that she does not think it was her or her brother. She is so grown-up and often replies, 'It's OK, Mommy, I love you and I'll take care of you, OK?'

It is possible for someone to 'pick up' on another even though they are in a coma. Some psychics can do this. When my own dear father was in a coma we chatted to him every day as if he were aware and awake. I always felt that if you hypnotized him, all our conversations would still be stored in there somewhere!

Other children seem to be able to chat to their departed brothers and sisters. Ria told me that she has two 'spirit children' and that her little girl regularly has conversations with them. She also plays with them! How much of this is 'imagination' is sometimes hard to tell, but of course in some cases the parents haven't even told their living children they have lost children to the 'other side'. It makes you wonder, doesn't it?

Chatting to Other Spirit Visitors

Not all of our special spirit friends need to be relatives. Serena's caller was like a kindly grandmother.

Mrs Coleson

From the age of six I used to sit facing the corner of my room at the left side of my bedroom window, and play or chat away to 'myself'. My mum used to pop her head around the corner of my door and say, 'Who are you talking to?'

I used to reply, 'That nice lady there, Mrs Coleson. She is reading me a story.'

My mum used to just smile and walk away. Then one day I spoke to my mum about my visitor in front of a neighbour. The neighbour went white and gasped, and told my mum that a woman called Mrs Coleson had died in our house several years before! To me she had always been real anyway!

I sometimes feel her presence now, but since my granddad passed away he is always in and out. I would love to have found out more about Mrs Coleson, but when I think about her I feel secure and warm inside.

Healing and Special Insight

Children seem to have such amazing understanding of life, don't they? Clodes explains:

I was experiencing a few personal problems, and one day my young nephew came to visit me. I was trying to keep my emotions in check, but he stood really close to me. He told me that it was a shame I couldn't stay longer in my job and that work 'were mean' because they wouldn't give me more time off work. He then looked at me and said, 'You'll be OK,' and he hugged me.

I told him he was a beautiful, special boy and I loved him very much. Hugging him made me feel warm and so strong again, and I could sense warm light from him but I couldn't see anything. If you look into my nephew's eyes, they are so big, soft and wise. They do not look like the eyes of a seven-year-old child at all.

My sister's son is remarkably intuitive for his age. At the age of three he announced to my sister that when people die they get given a new body and come back to Earth. How does he know these things?

My sister's neighbour had a dog with a brain tumour, that had to be put down. My nephew went over to the house and seemed to get upset. He was holding the dog's head. He truly didn't know that the dog had been put down. He then announced calmly to my neighbour that 'It's OK, Roo is in heaven now and the bad pain in his head is gone.'

There is no way he would have known about the brain tumour; it's as if he sort of picked it up from the dog.

Other Worlds and Planets

Is it possible that not only do our children come from other realms, but that they may still visit them? As we have discussed previously, Kathryn believes they do – and so do I. Kathryn worries that Allison gets scared of what she sees sometimes. Here is her story.

'Portal World'

Our daughter Allison has long visited what she calls 'Portal World'. This Portal World is located under her bed and she has two friends there. We often couldn't find her, which scared us, but we knew that as the youngest of four she also needed her privacy. She then explained that she had been visiting Portal World with Emily and Elizabeth. She often visited and told us fabulous stories (which we have since written down).

When she turned ten a few months ago, she cried her heart out because she said that once you turn ten, you are no longer allowed to visit Portal World, and she really missed her friends.

She has talked about it since, but now seems to have picked up a few abilities, too. She predicts things, things will fall without her touching them, and she still sees figures. Recently she saw a dark figure with red eyes, carrying a scythe (she drew a picture for us) but it frightens her. We have never showed fear of her 'abilities', nor discounted them, but now she is scared herself. I asked her if she had asked the figure what he wanted, and she said she was too afraid.

She quit telling her friends about this long ago, and now only speaks to her father and me about it. She thinks something bad is going to happen and sees this 'dark figure' (her words, not ours) at school. Our older daughter predicted her grandmother's death and often spoke to her after she passed away. She wasn't particularly close to her grandmother in life, but could tell us things about Grandma that I didn't even know, and only her father could confirm. As she got older and started to get into the social scene at school, she seemed to stop being able to do this. I think she still has the ability but hides it or maybe denies it to herself.

My mother recently had a biopsy and told no one but myself and her husband. Our older daughter told her that 'The doctor is going to call any minute now, and everything will be fine.' Nothing had been said when she was even in the house, so she couldn't have known. That is why I think she still has the ability!

Many of my readers have experienced portals or gateways to other worlds and realms. In fact, in a house where a lot of spiritual activity takes place (particularly where the activity is in one room or place), it may have some sort of portal where spirits are entering. If this phenomenon is troublesome, check out Chapter 11 for information and suggestions for closing down or managing the situation! I've said it before and I'll say it again – even if you don't 'believe' this stuff … it still seems to happen!

When I read this story I wondered if a portal might be in place here too … so varied is the activity!

Spirits in the House

My name is Tania and I am momma to four boys. Our youngest is 29 months old and has seen ghosts and spirits for a while now. I am aware that our home has some sort of spirit in it, but the signs come and go, and up until now I have been the only one bothered by these spirits. Usually they will wake me when I am sleeping, flicking my eyelids or floating around my head. Last night, however, our two-year-old awoke, insisting that a lizard was in our bed. After convincing him that there was not, he proceeded to talk about the dancing bear in the corner of the room and a frog of some sort who was saying bad words to him. After a minute or two he got very excited about the little boy who was standing at our bedroom door playing peek-a-boo with him. He said this little boy was hanging on the door and climbing the walls, although I guess he could have just been continuing on his dream ...

He kept pointing and saying, 'See, mom, there he is ...' and laughing at the bear who was apparently dancing for him. After we tried to settle him down a bit, he would sit back up and have conversations with the young boy he could see. I asked him what the boy was doing and he said, 'He is talking to me, Momma, he talks to me all the time!'

I went cold and I had the feeling of pins and needles all over my body. I proceeded to pick Lucas up and we stood exactly where he was seeing the boy. I told Lucas to ask the little boy to leave because he had to go back to sleep, and when he did he said the little boy said a bad word to him. I then asked the little boy to leave and Lucas said, 'Momma, he is saying bad words to you now, too.' As you can imagine, I was pretty freaked-out and turned the light on.

After gathering myself and waking my husband to tell him what had happened, we all fell back to sleep. In the morning when Lucas woke up he went to the door where he had seen the little boy and called for him!

Levitation and Dimensional Travelling

Levitation is the lifting or moving of an object or person by 'psychic means'. Several of the parents who have written to me have mentioned this as an ability they have witnessed in their children. Others have seen their psychic kids in more than one place at once or moving very quickly. Almost too weird to believe … but yet it happens.

Speedy Traveller

My daughter's friend (who has very high functioning autism and a very high IQ) has been discovered in one place, then seconds later somewhere else. How do you explain these things?

My friend's cousin was living at my mate's for a while, and her cousin saw this little girl (aged three) in her room, then seconds later saw her outside playing with a garden hose. When my mate checked the room, the girl was still there, so she peered outside again and she was no longer playing with the hose … she can travel that fast, within seconds. The whole incident left my friend shaking her head and saying, 'What the heck?'

I can imagine! Then another mum, Lynne, says that she hears her daughter walking around the house but then when she goes to check on her, finds her fast asleep in bed. She says also that a friend of hers has a daughter who can levitate, and believes it is one of the traits of the new children whom some people call 'Rainbow Children'.

Out-of-body Travellers (OBE)

At the point of death, near-death experiences and some-times during stress, the spirit appears to leave the body, to separate. This is commonly called an 'Out-of-Body Experience'. You may have heard of this, as it can also happen during meditation and during some disciplines like yoga. I've actually had this happen to me and it was the weirdest thing to find myself floating about the house whilst my body was lying on the bed in my room! You never quite look at the world in the same way again after this happens. There are many books and websites about the phenomenon if you are interested in learning more.

Of course, I wasn't at all surprised to hear that out-of-body travel was common with my psychic-children case studies! This is Susan's case.

High Flyer

We have had a couple of 'incidents' with our son, which have baffled my husband and myself. My son told my husband where his lost wrench was when he was five. He was not with my husband when he misplaced it, and told him it was at a location my son had never visited but my husband recognized immediately by the descrip-tion. It was at his friend's barn. My husband had been working there the previous weekend. When we asked our son how he knew where it was, he said he 'sensed' it. We didn't even know he knew the word 'sensed', let alone was able to use it in a sentence.

Now he is six, and two weeks ago his little brother was with me while my elder son was on a field trip. I got a speeding ticket on my way to the store, and when I picked my elder son up from his field trip I said to him, 'You will never guess what happened to Mom today.' He just said, 'I know, you saw a policeman and he gave you a ticket.'

There was no way he could have known, but then he explained to me, 'Remember how I "sensed" that you got a ticket? Actually I was there, not the real me, the "invisible" me. I was in my car seat and I just closed my eyes on the bus and I was invisible in your car, Mom!'

The whole thing is more common than you would think, with many people having a spontaneous one-off experience of this sort. Many find themselves floating above their physical body when they are asleep, including my daughter when she was small. She sometimes used to 'float' down to the local park in her spirit or soul body during the night and meet up with a school friend to play on the local swings, or sometimes find herself floating over the top of her body or bobbing up and down on the ceiling above. Of course, her physical body was firmly asleep in bed whilst this was happening!

Some people use the term *astral projection* when out-of-body travel is used to visit other dimensions or planets.

Mary has encountered this phenomenon with her own child.

Fly Time

I have a 28-month-old daughter named Stella who sees and talks to spirits and angels, mostly our relatives that have passed over. When she was a baby she would look at the ceiling, babbling baby talk and smiling and laughing.

Now Stella is talking more and more and I have come to realize she is *very* connected to the other side and may be psychic. The latest thing she has told me is that she flies at night when she is asleep and goes to different places, which makes me think she may be astral travelling.

I have just started out trying to learn all about this stuff, so I don't know too much about it all. I never thought I would be raising a child like this, because I am a Christian, but it has taught me that I don't know everything about God. I do know that these gifts that children are experiencing have come from God and are not evil.

I know that as our children grow, so will we, and that as we will grow with our children and learn more day by day, so we can help them develop their gifts the best they can.

Monica's ten-year-old daughter has several psychic talents, and when her mum asked Sami if she had ever 'astral projected', she didn't even ask what it meant, just immediately answered, 'Of course!' The young girl then described some of her experiences, which all seemed to take place in their home.

Monica told me,

> I asked if she has ever gone anywhere else and she said she didn't know she could do that. Her sister (Caitlyn) is a year younger and asked Samantha, 'Where will you go next time?' and Samantha immediately screamed 'Disney World!' which made us all laugh.

A Vessel for the Other Side

Ever felt used? In the nicest possible way, of course! It seems like our children's guides and guardian angels are happy to use passing human souls (on their wavelength) to help them carry out their work.

Jackie was kind enough to share her own experience with me.

Guardian-angel Lady

> About ten years ago I was with a friend and three members of my family at an agricultural show. There were thousands of people at the event and I suddenly found myself walking a few steps behind the rest of the group. I got a real urge to go over to a huge tent that housed

the cattle pens … although I had no idea why. It did cross my mind that I might lose the rest of the group in the vast sea of people, but the urge was so strong that I didn't waste a second in getting over to a pen that was occupied by a huge white bull.

There was a group of people admiring the bull and a little girl of around five or six years of age, who had climbed onto the rails of the pen. I stood directly behind her, and just a split second later the girl lost her balance and started to topple into the pen with the bull. Her feet came up and I felt a thud under my breasts where her feet had caught me. I instinctively reached forward and caught the child by the waist and safely lifted her back over the rails. The pen was only about 12 inches wider than the beast, and there was no doubt in my mind that, had the child landed in the pen, she would have startled the beast and been seriously trampled, if not killed, that day.

She looked up at me wide-eyed, as she realized how lucky she had been. No one else had witnessed the drama, so I simply said to her, 'That was very dangerous …' before dashing off to find my group. It didn't take me long to realize that her guardian angel had used me to save her … but that was OK!

Psychometry

Psychometry is the ability to receive information from an inanimate object. Many psychics are able to pick up information from an item of jewellery, for example, or to pick up information from the walls of an old building simply by touching them.

I have tried this practice in my workshops, and even the doubtful will be amazed at the results that even a non-believer will pick up.

Give it a go. Here is what you do:

- First of all, tell your child (and their friends) that this is a game (in a way it is, so don't make any more of it than that) ... of course, this is fun for the parents too!
- Collect together objects which belong to you and your family – or parents of your children's friends. Jewellery, clothing and personal objects work well. Place them in a basket. Cover with a cloth.
- Get your children to each reach in and take an object (one at a time).
- Ask them what they see, feel, hear and touch.
- Write down everything they say!
- Compare notes with the owner of the object ... are they reading their energy and memories correctly from the object?

Older children might enjoy doing the exercise blindfolded ... and may get even better results.

Roxie told me about the experiences with her own son:

Surprise?

I have a three-year-old son named Drew. He has talked to 'imaginary' people since he was able to speak (which was very early, by the way). He was speaking full sentences at ten months, things like, 'I did it,' 'What dat noise?' etc.

I have always had a little bit of a gift myself (knowing when someone has died, being able to tell you what card is coming next in a deck, etc.) but I think Drew has a much greater gift.

I have caught him talking to someone named 'Michael' several times over the last year. I asked him who Michael is and he told me Michael is an angel. He talks all the time about his angel.

This week, with Christmas coming, I had bought Drew several presents. He has the ability to go to the tree, pick up any present and tell you what it is before he's opened it. He also did this with my mom's birthday gift and has done it in the past with other things when he was as young as 18 months old.

I asked him what he thought Santa was bringing him for Christmas and he told me 'a pirate ship'. That actually was his Santa present! I suggested Santa might bring something else, but he told me, 'No, just a pirate ship!'

It's all fascinating, isn't it? I know, like me, you are probably still saying 'What? How?'

OK, let's have a look at some of the questions that readers have presented me over the last few years. I've picked out a small cross-section from the many thousands of letters I receive. I know you will enjoy reading them.

CHAPTER 7

Questions

The most beautiful thing we can experience is the
mysterious. It is the source of all true art and all
science. He to whom this emotion is a stranger, who
can no longer pause to wonder and stand rapt in awe,
is as good as dead: his eyes are closed.

Albert Einstein

My postbag is filled with hundreds of questions about
children's paranormal experiences. Using my own experience and wide research, trial and error, and the helpful suggestions from the parents of psychic children who
form my online support group, we have found a variety
of things that work.

Each child is different, and ultimately it is the parent
or guardian who decides on what is best for *their* child.
Usually people write to me when they have no idea how
to begin to address the problem presented by the psychic
phenomena which are occurring to and around their
child. I am not a childcare worker nor a child-health

professional, but I am a mum and I understand how frightening these things can be for parents.

Your doctor or religious leader might be open-minded and brilliant ... or useless with these things. Your friends might have had similar experiences, but it's also likely that they won't have had. Although there are many thousands and thousands of children who are experiencing paranormal phenomena at this time, they might not be living in your neighbourhood. Thankfully, the Internet does draw people closer together. Some of the best 'experts' I have come across are the parents of the psychic children themselves!

I've mixed questions I get asked and those found in readers' letters along with my answers. You might find something useful here or be able to mix-and-match the answers.

There is no right or wrong way, and hopefully you'll be able to find some tips or things to try with your own children. And if you have other suggestions, I would love to hear from you!

Ghosts in the Bedroom

My child wakes up frightened at night because he says he can see a ghost in his room. What can I do?

Jacky's Advice

Many children wake up in the night. This might be caused by any number of reasons including nightmares or just the urge to visit the toilet. Every shadow is not going to be a ghost, but that doesn't mean that some sort of spirit activity isn't present in the room ... it just might be.

Keep an open mind, but do appear in command of the situation at all times. You are the adult and if you are not worried (or can appear unworried), then most likely your child won't be, either.

My first recommendation is that you listen to your child's explanation of what is happening. You don't have to agree or disagree, just listen. Your child will believe what he's saying is true, and that's scary enough, thank you! Stay matter-of-fact in your reaction.

I always find that introducing the idea of guardian angels at this stage is particularly useful (see later chapters for more on this). It worked beautifully with my own kids. After story time, settle your children and ask them to imagine white fluffy angel clouds filling the room. Tell them that this keeps out the ghosts (it will). Explain that an angel stands at each corner of the room (or guards the door) to keep away whatever is frightening them. Use appropriate language to explain this to your own child in a way that is suitable for his age.

From a paranormal point of view, I've discovered that inviting angels to protect your child from any annoying psychic activity he might be experiencing really does work (it's not just about child psychology) ... and will likely be the end of the problem completely.

Some children may benefit from choosing a picture of an angel to hang on their bedroom wall (try framing a birthday or Christmas card), or you can buy or make an angel figurine to sit on a bedroom shelf. This helps the child to envisage the protection.

I suggest if you have a choice of images that you consider a picture of the archangel Michael, who is usually pictured with his flaming sword of protection (but not if your child might be frightened by this). The archangel Michael is traditionally in charge of the 'heavenly armies' – see him as a sort of 'angel bouncer' or, for younger children, an angel police constable or even super-hero!

Empowering children in this way will give them great confidence, enabling them to sleep easier at night. Always let your child pick his own 'angel of protection' symbol if possible. You can buy angel gifts from most gift and card shops, New Age stores and over the Internet.

Case History

My daughter is almost three and has recently become scared to be in the room she shares with her older sister. She tells us that there is a man at the end of her sister's bed and he tells her that he likes princesses and birds. When we take her into the bedroom, she points to an area in the room (as if she is pointing at someone).

My daughter describes the man as tall with blonde hair and blue eyes. My husband's father died several years ago and we wonder if it could be him. We have not seen anything ourselves.

Is there anything that we can do to find out more without leading her with questions, and if there is something that we should be doing to also see this person?

Jacky's Advice

Your daughter is at the age when many children see spirits (pre-school). It is my experience that our loved ones (especially a child's late grandparents) come to visit their younger family members, just as they would have done in life.

They visit with love and their intent is definitely not to frighten the youngsters. I suggest you get out the family photo album and spread out some old family photographs as if to sort them. Some children can point out relatives they have never met and those that they have never seen photographs of. You won't be leading your daughter if you don't ask any questions.

Your reaction is important. Say something like, 'Oh, how wonderful that Granddad has made a special trip from heaven just to visit you. He was a lovely man!' Make your child feel special without going over the top about it.

As long as the visits are not causing a problem, then let them continue. You might never be able to see him yourself, of course – although you could certainly ask if he might try to make himself known! As adults we are even more likely to be scared, so be careful of what you wish for!

If the visits are a problem (even if the visitors are loving relatives) you can enter the child's bedroom at night-time and speak directly to the spirits concerned. Say something like, 'Sally loves it when you come to visit her, but please don't stay too late because it makes her tired the next day and she has school.' Set your conditions but stay polite as you would with any loving visitors to your home in the 'normal' realm. Older (or braver children) can set their own conditions.

I know it seems strange to talk to 'thin air', but trust me, these things do work and your spirit visitors will respect you!

Annoying Invisible Friend

I'm not sure if you can help, but I work in a school and we have a five-year-old boy (let's call him Sam) who has just started school and seems to have an imaginary friend. The current one is called Flybo and doesn't seem to be very nice.

Before Christmas Flybo was playing with the tinsel so I asked Sam what he looked like. He squashed his face with both hands and said, 'Like this and his head is spinning!'

Today we had a bad experience with Flybo not letting Sam do his work. Sam was frightened by this and was worried, even for someone else to talk to Flybo. This was also a frightening experience for the teachers involved. Can the spirits that visit us be bad?

Jacky's Advice

The child's doctor might have a different explanation for this, but it's always worth looking at the paranormal angle as well. It is possible that the young boy is very psychic. As a child I often used to accidentally tap into negative energies myself (really, they are annoying spirits who have not passed over to the light and often bother people who are aware of them ... usually nothing more than irritating, but it can get worse).

Whether we believe in these annoying spirits or not makes no difference. They still seem to pop up from time to time, and there are quite a lot of children who can see spirits, including the aggravating ones (sometimes more than one child can see the spirit at the same time). In the case of many children, this ability disappears around the age of five to seven.

As we have seen throughout the book, many young children can see and talk to relatives on the other side, too, passing on information to living relatives about things they did not know about in advance. This is real too, even though we try to ignore it. Of course, chatting to Grandma is very different to the experience you are talking about here, and I can understand how disruptive this might be.

What is useful in this situation is that the child is not happy about the energy either, so the solution can be fairly straightforward. First of all I would suggest that the parents are made aware of the phenomenon and that they are in agreement with and support any process to assist the problem. They may already be aware of it and also be wondering what to do. Together you can be stronger.

Although I am not a child therapist, I do have many hundreds of emails on the subject and members of my Forum report back on activities and the success they have in this field with their own children (it may be worth joining my Psychic Children Forum online and chatting directly with the parents involved, who may also be able to make other suggestions).

Things which have worked for others:

1. With the parents' permission, talk to the young boy about guardian angels. Maybe this is something which would be appropriate for the whole class as part of a religious investigation or similar. Show him a picture of the archangel Michael (the warrior angel in charge of the heavenly armies, who is normally pictured with a sword).

2. Explain how angels protect us, even reading angel stories if appropriate. Tell him (or the class) that they have their own guardian angel and they can ask this angel for help at any time.

3. Ask the boy what his own guardian angel's name is (he will probably give you a name immediately – or he may say Michael). If he says he doesn't know, get him to 'ask' the angel. Take the name seriously and from that point on talk about his angel using his name. He can draw the angel to help reinforce the power of the image. This might make a great class project too!

4. The next time he seems to have a problem with the spirit 'Flybo', call up the angel. Be casual and slightly annoyed about it (annoyed with Flybo, not Sam.) Say something like, 'Oh, how annoying that that Flybo is here again. We are fed up with him, aren't we? Ask [your guardian angel/archangel Michael/angel police] to take him away and put him in prison [child-speak for removing the spirit to a place of safely].

5. If the spirit reappears, be dismissive: 'Well, we are no longer bothered by him/ignore him because [name of guardian angel] is taking care of him now.' Do not appear afraid, just slightly bored by the trouble-some spirit – often by giving the energy too much attention we can give it power. Many churches have a division whose sole job is to remove negative enti-ties (exorcism), so do take this seriously. However, do not feel afraid because the phenomenon is very common and can usually be sorted out fairly easily.

The most important thing – and I can't stress this enough – is to work in conjunction with the parents. If the parents are dismissive of the phenomenon, then the solution is more challenging. It's much harder to work directly with the child if the parents are not 'on board'. If you have difficulties, ask your own guardian angel to help from a different angle!

These are some of the ways that my Forum members have coped with the phenomenon of annoying spirits. Decide if this is something you want to try or not. You might prefer to take advice from a local medium or ask at your local spiritualist church (numbers are in the phone book) and work with someone who can see the energy too (a medium is a psychic who can see, feel or hear spirit energy).

A child psychologist or doctor might dismiss the experience as imaginary and suggest other techniques (counselling) – although I do hear of more and more doctors who are themselves enlightened and open to other possibilities.

Each case is individual, so by discussing this with the parents you can best see how to help. In all cases I would suggest involving all carers if possible. Either way, the psychological 'trick' of giving the boy power over this entity (with a guardian angel or spirit guide) can sometimes be enough to remove it.

A general whole-class discussion about angels (which are part of many religions but also work outside religion) might be useful too – place a poster/picture on the wall as part of the project. This could also be a constructive way to empower all children, as well as create another form of protection in the classroom.

Naked Ghost?

I'm feeling very confused. My sensible, honest six-year-old has told me he has seen a spirit in his classroom. He'd been asking strange questions about blue spirits in the lead-up to telling me about this.

Years before, around the age of two or three, he told me about rainbows around people's heads (i.e. he could see auras and all the colours he described around people were accurate to their mental state at the time) and he saw two spirits then too. Then it all stopped. Now this, added to his lifelong fear of being alone in any room, makes me wonder if there is more he hasn't told me.

My son told me he was working quietly at school when he was aware of someone coming into the room and looked up. He described what he saw as a spirit, a man with his face turned away from him, just simply walking through the classroom. My son glanced down, looked up again and the man had disappeared, then he reappeared outside the classroom. What was interesting was my son wasn't sure if he was a spirit because he had shoes on! But he described the spirit, telling me, 'He had no clothes, he was just a very, very light blue with white, but I couldn't see his body bits like his belly button or willy!'

So I'm assuming the spirit was more a *form* of a body. I asked my son if he was scared and he smiled and said, 'Oh, no.' But then he wouldn't speak about it any more. Who is it? I worry that by supporting him I'm opening a can of worms!

Jacky's Advice

I did laugh at your son's description! You know I do believe that spirits are around us all the time, but that for the most part we can't see them. It seems that, in common with many people, when your son is in a relaxed state or 'daydreaming' he opens up his psychic vision. For that brief moment he was able to tap into the world that overlaps our own (like tuning in a radio to a particular station).

I doubt the spirit was anyone in particular, just someone walking on by. You can explain this to your son but I shouldn't let it worry you in any way at all. It may happen again or it may not.

Where Did Grandpa Go?

My son has been seeing my dad for as long as he could see and speak. He never met my dad in life because Dad passed away a week after my son was born. He has told us various things that have happened and what his grandpa has said.

He has obviously grown to love his grandpa very much, and in the past has been puzzled as to why we can't see him too. We explained to him that my dad is now an angel and lives in the stars.

One day he told me that Grandpa hasn't been to see him in a while and he misses him. Bedtime is when Grandpa used to visit before.

Could you advise me what to say to him if my father doesn't come back, so that I can help him understand and not be too upset? He's four years old. Thank you so much.

Jacky's Advice

It's strange how young children take these things in their stride – so much so that if the experiences stop they are upset!

It's hard to know how to help, but sometimes our loved ones are moving up and on in their own spiritual development and so are further from the Earth plane. It becomes harder for them to reach us (as if we are at the bottom of a deep swimming pool – they have to hold their breath for a long time to reach us at the bottom. If they move up to the higher realms it's as if the swimming pool becomes deeper – so further to go and harder to hold your breath! You get the idea!).

You could tell your son that Grandpa has meetings and is now visiting his friends in heaven (or having a party – because, in its simplest form, this is true! Imagine those big reunions in the sky!).

Grandpa will still be aware of your son, especially when he is needed , but your son probably won't see him so often (he's still there, but it's like he lives further away now). Perhaps a photograph of Grandpa by the bed will be comforting.

I hope this helps a little. He is a very lucky boy to have seen his grandpa at all. Do help him to keep these memories alive by talking about them often.

Useful Feedback

Here's a reply from someone who found the initial advice she received quite helpful. If you are having similar problems, her experience shows that it's worth sticking it out!

> I have emailed you before about my young daughter Caitlin and would like to say a big thank you. Caitlin wouldn't have a bath or sleep in her own bed because she saw people in her room. She also used to see a little spirit girl in the bath (who we discovered had actually drowned).
>
> Now, two months on, Caitlin happily goes into the bath and to bed on her own. Your advice was to tell me to ask the angels for their help, and I know they came straightaway.
>
> I am just emailing you to tell you that every night Caitlin, who's three, asks the angels to watch over her. Tonight I asked her if she had seen any angels and she told me, 'Yes, Mummy, I saw Michael.' She told me, 'He doesn't wear clothes but has one wing. His hair is blonde like mine and he has long hair too, not short like Uncle Tim's.' Caitlin tells me he also has a crown – but not a princess crown like hers.

To say I was shocked would be an understatement. How can a three-year-old girl describe an angel like that? Thanks to your help and advice, however, I've come to accept and even be grateful that my daughter is a happy and normal three-year-old who just happens to see another world that some of us can't.

Advice from the Psychic Children Forum

This woman is a valued member of my Psychic Children Forum on the Internet and experiences many psychic phenomena herself as well as with her children. She had tried all sorts of different coping strategies and is now quite an expert. I'm happy to pass on her very good advice.

Ignore Them or Pray

If my daughter sees a spirit at school, I suggest she just ignores it if possible, or tells it to go away. This usually works. At home, or with me, she can listen to the spirit or talk about it in a safe environment.

As a parent I try to be very nonchalant about it, which is oh-so-hard to do! Inside I'm dying to know what she is seeing and why, but I don't ask too many questions. I let her tell me in her own time, although I might ask a question or two if I can do so casually. If she doesn't want to discuss it, I drop the subject.

If she is being troubled in school I tell her to silently pray – and the same goes for when she is at home if the spirits are bothering her, so that the spirits go away. At home she can pray as loud as she wants, although this is difficult at school.

She knows that I am the main one to seek if she has questions, although to be fair I don't have most of the answers!

We both could not contain ourselves when I was teaching in a Baptist church around Thanksgiving one year. My daughter saw my mother's spirit, and she was so excited she started screaming, 'Mama, Mama, it's your mom … come here, it's your mom …!' I was apprehensive to say the least, because I had five Christian teachers talking with me at the time! She'd been playing happily but I saw the sudden shock and wonder in her eyes. I went to her immediately, but sadly I didn't get to share her vision. However, she described my mother perfectly. What's interesting here is that even I didn't know what my mother looked like before she died. I had to be told by a friend because I was unable to be with her at the time. My daughter's description matches perfectly what the neighbour described.

If children can learn to ignore the negative entities or tell them to go away (if the visit is at an inappropriate time) or learn my method (prayer), then the parents should help them to do this. The child needs to know that they have boundaries.

Going by experience is what worked best for us,

but I know some of you veterans out there will have lots more suggestions to add!

Monica is another regular member of the Forum. Her family are very 'together' and 'normal' about the paranormal experiences that are part of their lives.

Stay Normal

I've always been open with my children about my own abilities and encourage them to ask questions. The girls love being part of the paranormal world, and my son – even though he has never liked to draw attention to himself – I think he will become more excited the more he learns.

We all laugh about some of the crazy things that happen and none of the children has ever been scared. I know they trust me and know that they can always talk to me about anything without fear of judgement. They know I will answer their questions truthfully and honestly, and if I don't know the answer they know I will try to find it.

The girls thought I was the coolest thing since sliced bread when I made the whole electrical system in the house go nuts while they were here to witness it. This was just a week or so ago and it was the first time I had ever done that, so I am not sure if I'll ever be able to do it again or not. If I could control it, it would be a great party trick.

We all feel that these are gifts from God and that we are blessed. We also know that God would not give us these gifts unless they were positive gifts and meant to be used for good. We feel that since they are gifts from God, then there is absolutely no reason to fear them or the spirits that sometimes accompany them.

My children are confident, well-rounded, bright, active, spiritual and talented (musically and in acting, modelling, sport, etc.). They are very concerned about the environment, love animals and are not afraid to stand up for themselves and others when it comes to someone being wronged or treated inappropriately.

They have been through a lot of tough situations that most children never have to experience and hopefully never will. They have had to learn to deal with many adult situations. I am so very proud of my children! Yes they have psychic abilities, but I want everyone to know that these abilities are only a small part of who they are. Of course they are not perfect; they still act like normal children. They misbehave, don't clean their rooms or do their chores, 'forget' to do their homework, etc. and are punished accordingly with 'time-outs', grounding, loss of privileges, etc. So they are not treated any differently than if they didn't have these abilities.

I do wish that there was some type of support group or something we could join that could help them (and me) with developing our abilities. I've been aware of my own abilities since I was very young. I want them to have a better understanding of what's going on and not have to 'second-guess' their abilities like I did mine. Growing up and being psychic and seeing visions that I didn't understand was stressful and affected me physically.

My parents didn't approve of me talking about what I was going through. I can only assume they didn't understand and were ignorant of the difference between being 'crazy' and being psychic. As far as I know, I am the first psychic in my family. I think my parents were always afraid I might say something inappropriate about my visions and embarrass them in front of their friends.

Visit my website at www.JackyNewcomb.com to find out more about joining my (free) Psychic Children Forum.

I Need Help Now!

I have an 11-year-old daughter whom I believe has 'the sight' me and my mother have (as well as my grandmother and great-grandmother).

Her abilities do seem to be more frightening than normal. I have always allowed her to experience as much as possible where this is concerned.

When she has questions she always comes to me. We have lived in the Cincinnati area since early August and my daughter's room has been her place of dread since about the first week in September. While we were unpacking she loved it. Then she called me up into her room late one night with her eyes swollen. She was shaking like a leaf and asking me what it meant to see lights come out of her floor!

I stayed with her for the better part of an hour and didn't see a thing, yet felt all the while as if something was trying to avoid me.

I did a quick blessing, gave her a statue of a guardian angel and told her to tell the spirit to go away because she was trying to sleep.

Now, until recently, every time she's done this and said a little prayer she's been fine, but now this 'thing' will NOT leave her alone. We have performed smudgings with sacred white sage [see page 230], sprinkled cleansing sea salt and even performed blessings with holy water. My daughter says the happenings always wake her up and keep her awake. I told her two weeks ago to start a journal of everything she sees, hears, feels, etc … and she came up with this list over a few weeks:

- lights still coming out of floor
- hearing breathing, feeling breath
- Twiggy (the guinea pig) acting strange (she told me her guinea pig would start literally screaming and running around her cage, digging and trying to get out)
- sudden bad stomach pain
- sudden feelings of anger against everyone, but with no reason
- feeling tired but not allowed to sleep

- feeling 'them' make her leave the room
- hearing voices that do not belong to family
- hearing crashes and steps on the creaky stair but no one visually walking up them
- crying for no reason even though it's daytime and she's usually feeling happy
- tugging on pajamas at night and on clothes during the day
- toys moving
- stuffed animals looking angry
- door opening a little, though she locks it all the time
- bad 'photographs' (she says visions flash in her mind of pictures of bad things like angry people and animals)
- 'them' telling her to stop this list she's making!

I'm so worried for her. In my life I have never dealt with anything like this before. Any help would be very much appreciated.

Jacky's Advice

You have tried most of the things I would normally suggest, but you are right, you do need help. I suggest you contact either:

1. Your local church to ask for an exorcist to come and remove this spirit (if you feel this is right for you).
2. Your local spiritualist church and see if they have a member/team who deals with this sort of thing (or

a local medium may be able to help). The spirit will clearly not leave until its problems have been dealt with. It probably doesn't even know it is dead. Try your local New Age/crystal shop or people who advertise Reiki healing, that sort of thing. They may have local contacts you could try (get a recommendation if you can). There may be a charge.

Animals pick up a different vibrational energy from humans (similar to spirits), so the poor guinea pig will feel like someone is shouting in the room! Clearly this is a bigger problem than is easy to deal with on one's own.

Do keep smudging the room, though, because it is much harder for the spirits to manifest in a room full of sage. (See Chapter 9 for more detail on this!) Try also using an oil-burner in the room (when your little girl is not in there, for safety's sake). To the water (in the well at the top of the burner) add two or three drops of pure frankincense oil (health food shops, New Age stores or the Internet will sell this). Frankincense oil raises the vibration of the room, making it easier for angels and higher-energy beings to come in and help. It is a little expensive, so buy the smallest bottle you can find as you won't need much.

My Two-year-old Is Driving Me Nuts!

I know through your column and websites you are very busy, but I was hoping you would take time out to read my letter, also maybe offer some guidance.

Jacky, my request is quite an unusual one. You see, it's my wee daughter Katie. She has the will of iron and never gives in or says sorry. I know she is just a baby, but she knows the difference between right and wrong. If she is misbehaving and we see her doing so, after she has finished she will get up and walk up to her room. I've put her in her room and taken away her favourite toys but to no avail.

If I try to speak to her in a stern tone she just says, 'Don't speak to me like that,' ... and she's just two years old! Katie is a happy child, Jacky – as long as things go her way. If not, she just lashes out.

I feel that she is going to break me. She sleeps with me and won't go with anyone else, not even her dad. If I go out she sits at the door, screaming, until I return. The childcare centre asked me to remove her after four sessions, saying she was still too attached to me. I feel she is slowly draining the life out of me.

The other and major reason I'm emailing you is that I live in a flat that has two floors. Since Katie could speak, if we were upstairs and someone knocked on the door, she could tell me who it was. The same before you got to the phone. At first I didn't take much notice, until Katie told my friend Margo (who has had infertility problems) that she has a baby in her stomach. I told Katie that she was wrong but Katie insisted. Jacky, this persisted for about eight weeks and Katie would repeat this every time she saw Margo. Later, at her diabetes clinic, a blood test proved Margo was indeed pregnant!

With Margo and with my other friend, Donna, who is also having a baby, Katie would go to their stomachs and say, 'Bob the Builder in there.' I asked her what she meant and she said, 'Boy babies.'

At a scan six weeks later Margo discovered she was having a boy, and Donna found out the same information ten days later. Katie also told us as she was falling asleep one night that our neighbour Debbie was in a car crash. I checked, but luckily she hadn't been. Then, two days later, she was. The car was a complete write-off. When Debbie came to my house afterwards, Katie said to her, 'Driving too fast, eh?'

Jacky, I would be glad of any guidance you have to offer.

Jacky's Advice

It sounds like you have your hands full! Yes, your daughter is very psychic and the problem is that a lot of these children are old souls and have been here many times – they forget in this lifetime that they are children again!

I know it is a pain, but for her own sake and yours you have to lay down some rules – and *now*. Do you watch the super-nanny programmes on TV? The kinds of methods they use would help a lot. You could also ask for help from your local health visitor (attached to your doctor's surgery). There are many parents of children who are not psychic who will still recognize the other symptoms you describe as 'the terrible twos'. Children of this age love to establish the rules around them, but we as parents have to take charge … this too shall pass! (Eventually.)

My own daughter used to get out of bed and scream every night to be allowed back downstairs. We bought a stair gate and blocked off the top of the stairs. She got out of bed, we put her back. Out she came and we put her back – again and again and again. Often she would fall asleep on the landing! We'd pick her up and put her into bed. Finally she got the hang of it. They do, you know!

You need some persistence in your rules and need for other family members to back you up. Please do not feel I am criticizing you in any way (I promise you I am not). When one of my daughters was this age and I was potty-training her, I remember writing in my journal, 'This is the worst day of my life …' YES, that bad! I can look back and laugh now at my two beautiful and talented teenage girls. You have to stand firm in your rules and not let her break you. Otherwise the poor thing will really struggle at school and her life will be difficult.

Discuss the new rules with some close family and friends. Do one at a time and then tell your daughter what the rule is. Keep with that rule until she gets it. Number One rule is that MUM is in charge (children do need boundaries and YOU know this already). Take plenty of time out for yourself too. You deserve a break.

Do not let other adults call her 'difficult' or 'naughty'. If she does ANYTHING well, praise her in front of others. 'What a good girl for doing what Mummy asks … what a good girl you are for picking up your doll … well done,' etc.

Start a 'star chart', with stars awarded for EVERY good deed (buy stacks of these – show people what a good girl she is by sharing her star chart with others. Get your friends and family to back you up with comments like, 'Mummy tells me you are a good girl and always go to bed at night,' etc. This traditional behaviour-management stuff works just as well with psychic children as it does with your average toddler!

Bad behaviour should mainly be ignored, but set up a 'time-out' step or corner. You make the child sit or stand there for one minute for each year old they are if they misbehave. If they've made a mess, they also still have to clean it up/apologize, etc. after their 'time-out'. Make sure that good behaviour is rewarded with plenty of your time ('Let's do a puzzle,' etc.).

You must also get her used to being away from you. Leave her with a sitter for just a few minutes at a time at first, and praise her when she is good. She will soon lose the anxiety when she knows you always come back. Give her something of yours to look after while you are away (an old purse which you take out of your bag. Something she thinks is important and you are trusting her with).

OK, that's got some of the normal stuff out of the way – but the psychic stuff seems real enough too. One of the games you could play with her might be psychic development games, though of course you call them 'guessing games'. Make some up ... throw a dice and see if she can guess what number it will be. Look at photographs and 'make up stories' about the people in them. You get the idea ... all these games are for when she is a 'good girl', though, not for when she's being bossy or rambunctious.

Make sure she does not get over-tired, hungry, thirsty, etc. These all bring about negative behaviour. At this age, to be honest, all kids are a pain (mine sure were). But you *can* get through this. You sound like a great mum, so stand firm and ride out the storm. Your daughter sounds like she has the potential to be a great psychic one day.

Of course, if you discover other things that work for your psychic child, write and let me know so I can pass them on to other families and carers! Good luck.

Teaching Kids

I would like to ask about what you feel about children under the age of 16 sitting in on psychic development circles. I belong to a spiritualist movement and sit in circles myself, but part of the movement is run by the SNU (which is the Spiritualists' National Union) and they have their own code of practice. However, we are an independent church, and myself and a friend (who is a medium) feel there is a need for children – especially the Indigo and Crystal children – to develop and sit in a development circle of their own.

We have had a few people ask, but our minister doesn't agree with it. I understand his concerns for protection, etc. and with children being innocents, but if we look at mediums in the past, many started with their mother's circle at a very early age.

I have taught my son, who is 12, to protect himself. I also send the protection out to all three of my children and my home every night. I just wondered what your thoughts are on this.

Jacky's Advice

I guess that depends on the child! Perhaps if there are several parents and kids who are interested, they could set up their own development groups with the parents taking it in turn to hold a class. Or each parent takes it in turn to host a group in their own home with the parents and the kids taking part (group meditation, teaching them about things like psychometry, etc.).

I once had an 11-year-old girl in my angel group (accompanied by her dad) and she more than held her own. My own kids knew about psychic protection from the earliest age. I think it's time to stop 'protecting' children from the love of spirit and start teaching them! Knowledge is power, but as always, the parents must decide what is best for their own children.

How Can I Help My Son?

I am currently reading your book *An Angel by My Side* and although I'm not much of a reader your short stories and accounts suit me fine.

My nine-year-old son has started to see spirits. At first he saw a dog but only its head, and he told me it looked sad. I said if it visits again to say hello to it and maybe that it was looking for its owner.

Then the other day in our lounge he walked through the door and was a little taken aback. I asked him if he was OK and he said that there was a tall thin man there for a second or two and that the man was wearing a white polo shirt and jeans. How can I help him to develop his ability?

I myself have had dream-visits and returning-into-my-body experiences. My son is dyslexic but of very high intellect and I wondered if this was why he was more perceptive of our visitors.

I am hoping you can help me to help him.

Jacky's Advice

What a supportive mum you are! Just continue to do what you are doing. Ask him about what he sees, and tell him that a lot of people can see spirits and what a special gift it is (in the way that some people might be good at singing or playing football).

If he can talk to you openly about it, it will help him to keep his skills active and growing. Read as much as you can about mediumship and psychic protection and phenomena, and then you'll be ready with the answers to his questions.

Keep up the good work.

Protection in Dreams

I have a son, Robert, who is 'special needs' and he keeps having these recurring dreams that now seem to be up-setting him. He tells me that he dreams in colour and that there are these Aztecs/Native Americans chas-ing him. When they appear, he tells me that his dream changes to black and white.

Robert tells me that he is trying to get away from them, but they are coming into the house. He shuts the door on them but they walk through the door. Robert has said that he feels he knows one of them. He said he is frightened as he does not feel that he is in control of his dreams any more. He is getting so that he doesn't want to go to bed because of these dreams, and appar-ently he has had them for years but has only just told me about them.

I don't know if this will have any bearing, but I saw a clairvoyant last year and she told me a few things about Robert. She said that he has an old head on young shoulders; he is quite an 'old soul'. She said he is very special to the spirits, a very spiritual child (an Indigo Child). She said that he is drawn to crystals and that, because of his knowledge of them, Robert will be drawn to 'vivid' crystals; he will work with them and become a healer in the future. (Robert actually told me last year that he could see my aura; he told me the colour that was surrounding me.)

She also told me that Robert will start to talk about Buddhas and Tibetan monks and Amerindians, as he has been with them in a past life. She told me that he has guides and helpers but they won't come forward yet as he is a little too young. She informed me that Robert will come out with 'some strange things', and that he is getting very spiritual.

Now because of this dream I am aware of what Robert has had for Lord knows how long. I am quite concerned, unnerved, not quite sure how to put it into words, and I'm also not sure how to deal with it.

Part of me is wondering if it is just an overactive imagination. Another part is questioning if it could be someone trying to contact him (and for what reason?). And why on earth did Robert say that this Native American was someone he recognized? Robert does seem confused about this himself.

Have you come across anything like this before, Jacky? Or are we totally off our trolley? I would love to hear your views.

Jacky's Advice

No, you're not off your trolley! This might be something to do with 'past lives' or any number of things. It almost doesn't matter because, either way, you can do things to help.

First of all, Robert is not too young to have his 'guides' or 'guardian angels' step forward, because many readers write and tell me about their children's guides. May I suggest that together you find an angel picture or painting/postcard and get it framed for his room? This will help him (and you) visualize protection from whatever is scaring him.

As he is good with crystals, you could take him to a crystal shop and get him to choose a crystal which will protect him whilst he sleeps (tumbled stones – where the natural sharp edges have been softened and polished – are cheap, so that way you could pick up two or three of the same stone if necessary so you always have spares). Place the stones in a dish by the bed or under Robert's pillow if you want – whatever feels right to you both. Get your son involved in making these choices.

He can ask for his angel to help him at night, and he can ask for the angels to get the dreams to stop. Get him to visualize himself in a super-being type of outfit (Spider-Man/Superman type of thing, whatever is his favourite); this will stop him getting hurt or feeling hurt in his dreams.

Tell him to take an army of angels with him into his dream (remind him each night: 'Don't forget to take the angels with you tonight … remember that nothing can hurt you when they are around …' etc.).

The more of this sort of thing you do, the more empowered Robert will become – trust me, this stuff works. I'm sure you will find this helps a lot.

How Do We Deal with Her Psychic Gift?

I really just need your advice for my three-year-old granddaughter. She has seen two spirits so far and it really is scary for her. She starts to well up with tears and has to be taken out of the room.

Please could you advise me as to what we can say so she won't be so afraid? We have told her she is very special to see people and also to speak to them, but she is too young to understand and gets very tearful when we mention it.

Please can you help? I know you must be very busy and I love your books.

Jacky's Advice

Thank you for your email. It sounds as if you are all doing brilliantly already, so keep up the good work. You are already on the right track. As with all things, your granddaughter needs to know that her 'elders' know and understand what is going on and are 'in charge'. So I suggest the following:

1. Read as much as you all can. Be knowledgeable.

2. Be as down to earth about it as you can: 'Oh, goodness, loads of people around the world can do this … I wish I could …' etc.

3. Say things like, 'These people just want to say hello …'

4. Once she is comfortable in the fact that she is protected and safe, show her (tell her) how she can ask her guardian angel to remove people if she does not want to talk to them. Her guardian angel can also act as a 'gatekeeper' and only let in the nice spirits (this all helps her to feel empowered). Practise this with her – all the while seeming very down to earth about it. Let her know that you are totally cool with it all. 'See' the angel telling off the spirits or asking them to leave (whatever she will understand).

5. Ask her what her guardian angel is called (let her make something up – or she might actually GET the name directly – either way it doesn't matter). Start talking about your own guardian angel (make up a name). Talk to your angels together.

The more normally you treat this, the better she will handle it. Kids learn to deal with anything – going to the dentist, school exams, etc. This will have a payback for you in the long run. You can tell her that her guardian angel can hear her when she talks to him/her like a special friend whom she can share secrets with. Many children can already communicate with angels in this way – and more so after being told they can.

Thank you so much for this great question.

Who Makes the Noise?

Last night we had a spirit visit. My daughter Alex said it was in her room and made a high-pitched screeching noise all night long. It terrified her. She was too scared to tell it to leave, and too scared to get up and get me. It kept her up all night long, throwing things around her room and making this noise.

She called on her late grandpa and the screeching noise stopped, but the spirit didn't leave! Her room was a wreck this morning. It pushed all the buttons of her alarm clock, took the cable cord off her TV, and threw clothes and stuffed animals all over.

I had both of my kids in the car this afternoon. I asked Alex if the spirit was a male or female, when to my surprise it was my 12-year-old son who answered, and said it was a boy! Alex said he was aged around seven years old. 'No!' Dylan said. 'He's more like four!'

'Yeah, you're right, Dylan, he is closer to four,' said Alex, agreeing! They discussed the 'visitor' and came to the conclusion that he was crying and throwing somewhat of a tantrum because Alex was not communicating with him.

'Didn't you hear the noise he was making all night?' Alex asked me. 'It was sooo loud.'

I never heard anything. Dylan said the spirit boy came into his room and was moving things around. Do you think my son has psychic abilities, too? I have been more focused on my daughter. But when I spoke to my grandpa through the medium, he said, 'I will always be there to protect BOTH of your children.' I'd appreciate your input.

Jacky's Advice

The minute things start to become disruptive it is time to consider whether it's worth getting professional help to remove the spirit. I can't tell you what to do (and it is not my place) but I could tell you what I would do if it were my own child:

1. I would ask my child to communicate with the spirit one last time and say that they are not allowed to play at night-time when they are meant to be asleep.
2. I would ask my child to say that messing up the room is not allowed either. They aren't going to change their minds because the spirit child is naughty.
3. I would ask the spirit boy about his own guardian angel – it might bring in a spirit guardian or spirit parent who would be able to help remove the child spirit completely (… strange but true!).

It does seem as if both of your children can see the spirit child, but there is a big difference between a spirit visiting as a fun playmate (or helper) and one who is disruptive and making a mess, right? The same rule would apply to an 'Earth-living' visitor! A badly behaved friend would be asked to leave too!

Night-time Visitors Are a Pest

My son has never been a good sleeper, and often wakes through the night, especially around the hours of two to three a.m. My parents live a few doors away and have exactly the same kind of house. When my son sleeps at their house in the identical bedroom, he sleeps all night long without waking.

I have actually asked him about this a few times; on the first occasion he told me that at our house there is a man who visits him in the night and wants to play with his toys. This same spirit doesn't go to his grandparents' house ... no toys there!

I have recently started to attend a spiritualist church and was advised to explain to my son that this is an angel and that, whoever it is, it will not harm him in any way.

I have tried this but would be grateful if you can tell me whether to keep discussions to a minimum or try to encourage him to talk so we can try and explain things to him. Sometimes (I think it is due to his age as well) when we start talking he just sits and laughs, but then at other times he tells me there is not just an old man but children too.

I would be grateful for a response if you get the time – and just to say I bought one of your books recently, and it is now 'doing the rounds'. I had never actually read or seen any of your books before this incident. So, to whomever or whatever, thank you.

Jacky's Advice

First of all, thanks! I'm glad you enjoyed reading my book!

These night-time visitors can be a problem, even when they are friendly! I don't think these visitors are angels, and it would be confusing to tell your son that they are. It is common for spirits (mainly late relatives) to visit children at night, and also for spirit children to visit, as they do indeed like to play with our children's toys!

I suggest a regular routine of reading a bedtime story. Then say goodnight to the room (visitors!): both of you say something like, 'Goodnight, God bless, see you in the morning … don't wake me up, please, because I need my sleep!' Sometimes just asking the spirits not to wake the child can be all that it takes!

The spirits should get the hint! If your son is happy with the visits you could suggest to the spirits that they can come at the weekend when it's not a problem for school and so on.

❖❖❖❖❖❖

So there you go ... some of the weird and wonderful things that parents are dealing with right now. Confusing? Certainly scary! Some of my answers are similar, so by now you may be familiar enough with them to be able to use them in your own household if you need to.

Of course, if you are not the parent or relative of a psychic child, it does still make fascinating reading! OK, let's go and have a look at the phenomenon of 'past lives' ... you'd better read it to believe it!

CHAPTER 8

Past Lives

Children who remember their past lives offer the most
compelling evidence yet for reincarnation ...

Carol Bowman, *Children's Past Lives*

Other Lives?

Many children around the world have memories of 'past
lives'. They 'remember' their soul living lives in other
bodies; sometimes these are earthly lives and occasionally lives in other realms or planets. These memories aren't
always full ones. Sometimes a fragment of 'memory' will
leak into their normal everyday consciousness. For example, one little boy was at an air show with his parents
when he recalled a past-life memory. His told his startled
parents, 'Once when I was big I flew a plane but then
another plane shot me down and I died ...'

Is there anything to these memories? Many research-
ers believe there is. Much research has gone into investigating cases of past-life memories, and one researcher at

least believes he has proved the existence of many lives lived by each soul. Dr Ian Stevenson is widely acknowledged as the founder of scientific research into reincarnation. He has travelled thousands of miles to research cases of children remembering previous lives, often visiting remote places around the globe. He regularly had to work with an interpreter, travelling back to the same regions over and over again to meet all the relevant people in the story. He visited such places as Africa, Alaska, British Columbia, Burma, India, South America, Lebanon and Turkey to follow up children's claims. Many of his cases, and his extraordinary findings, have been published in over 200 articles and several books including *Children Who Remember Previous Lives: A Quest of Reincarnation*.

There are some other great books on the subject. I especially enjoyed *Children Who Have Lived Before* by Trutz Hardo and *Children's Past Lives* by Carol Bowman.

The younger the child, the stronger these memories seem to be. As soon as they can talk, children seem to mix up previous and current lives. Youngsters recall family members who don't exist … in this lifetime at least … and places that they have never visited before.

Often the child will go into great detail about the work that they did in a previous life – and even tell you how they died! For the unaware parent it causes great confusion! Children usually take it all in their stride. These memories often surface during relaxed times, and their comments are casual and offhand as the memory has just come to mind.

These memories often fade as the child gets older, and sometimes they forget their random comments shortly afterwards … but not always!

Laura is from Edinburgh in Scotland. Here is her story.

Do You Remember Before?

My little girl had lots of problems before birth, and then again immediately afterwards, which continued for the first few weeks of her life. I believe this has made her a very special child with a gift that others don't usually have.

When she was tiny she used to lie in her crib with her hands clasped each night as if she was praying. It was really cute but as she got older and started to talk she would say the strangest things. She would talk about people I had never heard of, and regularly mention old-fashioned names that are hardly in use these days.

Then one day we were sitting together having some quiet time when she quite happily said, 'Mummy, do you remember when you were not my mummy? I had another mummy before.'

I told her I had always been her mummy, but later on that evening when I had thought about it a bit more I wondered if she was talking about what people call 'past lives'.

She is now seven and a half and rarely talks about anything unusual these days. Maybe because she is getting older.

Sue's son Connor was chatting away to his mum one day when he casually commented, 'Wouldn't it be funny if you were my son, Mum?' An interesting thought! Apparently, he also remembers that he was once an old man named Sam!

Connie told me about her son Declan.

The House with the Yellow Door

I shall try to begin from where I first noticed things that were different about our son. We were driving down a road which myself and my husband had driven down numerous times before ... but never with our son, who was then nearly three. Declan looked at me and said, 'Mummy, this is the road that I used to live on with my mummy, not *you*, Mummy, but my other mummy ... it was just me and my other mummy that used to live here, until she went away, then I went away too.'

At first my husband and I didn't know what to say, so we just looked at each other. Then, before I could ask him any questions, Declan said, '... the house with the yellow door,' (may I point out that he had not learned his colours yet) at which point we drove past an old-looking but normal terraced house with a yellow door.

My husband and I just looked at each other, aghast! I asked my son, 'What do you mean, babe? In that house … not with Mummy and Daddy?'

'Yes, that one, but it wasn't *you*, Mummy, it was my other mummy. The mummy I had before you were my mummy. I was old and so was my mummy, but then she went away and so did I … and then I came to you.'

We were quite taken aback, as you can imagine, and asked no more questions until we were at home later that evening. Once my son had gone to bed we asked each other, 'How, what, why …?', but we could find no explanation.

Then, maybe a month or so later, we were driving back down this particular street when Declan said in quite an upset tone, 'Mummy, my door has changed, it's not yellow any more.' Then he went very quiet. We drove further along the road and found that the door had indeed changed … it was no longer a yellow wooden door but a white double-glazed one. He hadn't even seen the door when he mentioned it.

Declan has not mentioned his 'other' mummy since then and he's is now six and a half, so I wonder if he has forgotten.

Back Again

Author Carol Bowman has written an excellent book, *Return from Heaven: Beloved Relatives Reincarnated Within*

Your Family. I have come across this strange phenom-enon, too. Here is an unusual story from my case files.

Here I Am Again

This is a bit of a strange one for me. Our family is a little bit psychic but this really floored me.

I have a very close bond with my grandson, which was evident from birth. I had custody of him for almost a year due to family problems, and when he was given back to his mother she disappeared (on the run from police and family services) for two years.

In that time Tyrone would 'call me' psychically. Each time, I would then get a call from family services not long after. He was 20 months old when his mother took off with him for two years.

His mother and I are now in contact and I'm pleased to say we have resolved our past issues. I get to see my grandson on a regular basis, and he often stays with me for a week or more at a time.

Strangely, my grandson keeps calling me 'Mum' and telling me I'm his mother. Of course, I always correct him and say I'm his 'oma' (grandma), but he tells me I am both his mummy and his oma.

I usually leave it at that, but then three weeks ago whilst I was putting him to bed he started to tell me this strange story. He said, 'When I was in your belly, Oma, a long thin stick thing came and got me in the head [showing me his forehead] and it did kill me and then I did come back to my daddy and mummy, but this time I came back as a boy.'

    I was stunned. The eerie part was that 22 years ago I had a termination. It's left me wondering, has the child that I aborted all that time ago come back to me now? I just find it a strange thing for a four-year-old to say.

It makes you wonder, doesn't it? If a child is meant to be with a family, he or she will certainly find a way.

Carol Bowman has a fabulous story in her book, *Return from Heaven*, which describes how a young girl would talk regularly to her deceased stepbrother on her toy telephone. Tragically, Roger had died in a car accident, but his young stepsister Lauren communicated with him after he had passed on.

Roger's step-mum Nadine tells Carol how her daughter Lauren would chat away to Roger on her pink toy phone, regularly pausing as if listening to the other side of the conversation. These conversations were filled with much laughter and fun.

Then one day Lauren announced that Roger was coming back again. It seemed a strange thing to say at the time, but it may be that Lauren was right: Nadine's son Donald was born a year later and, according to doctors, 'against all odds'.

As soon as he was old enough to talk, Donald began recalling the car accident as if it had happened to him personally, along with many other events that had happened to Roger when he was still alive.

Carol's book contains many more intriguing stories and I highly recommend it.

Pre-birth Memories

My files do contain a few rare cases of adults remembering a life before life, a time when they (as souls) resided in the heavenly realms ... a time before they were born.

Many more children have these memories too. According to these testimonies we not only pick the lives we are currently living but we *choose* the families we'll live with once we are born. They're usually souls we have lived with over many lifetimes, to be reborn with again in the same family unit or as close family friends. These are called our 'soul groups'. Of course, this might explain how we are instantly attracted to some people ... and perhaps why we just as instantly dislike others!

Sarah wrote to tell me about her son Michael, and then later they emailed me together about Michael's experiences.

Before I Was Born

Michael told me, 'I remember choosing my family as soon as I was out of my buggy. I couldn't tell anyone because I didn't have the knowledge to put it into words. I am ten years old now and as I have got older and learned more expressive words I have been able to tell my mam more.

Before I was born I remember being in a room in heaven. It was a large space and very colourful. There was a man standing behind a big book. I stood opposite him, facing the book, and opened it. I looked at the pictures of the families that I could choose from and the pictures moved like a film, but really fast.

Nobody in the book spoke but I felt warm and fuzzy when I chose the family I wanted to be with. When I chose my family, I said goodbye to the man and a really bright light came down and I was told I would forget everything about this place when I got to the bottom. I was sad when I was told I would forget.

When I was travelling in the light, I kept telling myself that I wanted to remember, and I did! Then I felt warm as if I had just put on my dressing gown on a cold day. I was in my mam's tummy. I was all squashed up and it was a dark pink colour all around me. It was warm and I could hear some squishing noises.

The place I was in before I was born was calm and peaceful. There were lots of other people there, and nobody was sad. It was colourful and warm. There were flowers and buildings and they looked clean, not polluted like they are on Earth. I knew that there would be one other person in my family that I already knew. I didn't know if it would be a boy or a girl because it was Aime's choice whether to be a girl or not [Aime is Michael's sister]. Everybody gets to choose for themselves.

The people I left behind were friendly and talkative, nice, just like you want people to be. I don't remember eating anything in heaven but I'm not sure if I did. People told me that they would see me when I was on Earth but that I might not recognize them. They would be people that would help me and be my friends. My friend, Dominic, used to be a solicitor before he came back here this time.

My sister and Dominic are part of the same soul group as me, and so are my friends Nathan and Jeremy. They don't remember me from before they were here and that's a bit sad because I can't do anything about that.

As well as Dominic, I have a really close friend called Emily and I remember being with her in another life too. I don't know if we were married, but she was a big part of my past life, and she is a big part of my life now. I have known her since I first went to nursery. She is always happy, like me. In my past life I was male. I know I lived in this country but I am not sure where.

That's about all I remember but I talk to my gran (who is in heaven) and she has told me the answers to some questions in school.

My sister has had some experiences too, not of pre-birth but of spirits coming to her. Our house always has weird things going on all of the time, but it's cool, not scary.

Similar experiences to Michael's can be found in the books *Journey of Souls* by Dr Michael Newton and *Between Death and Life* by Dolores Cannon.

Kim's son seems to remember a time before he was born, too.

When I Was with Jesus

Tonight my son asked me if I miss Dad (we've been divorced for nearly three years.) I told him no and he asked why. I reminded him that Dad's not too nice to me, so no, I don't miss him. I told him I miss (and I named my boyfriend). He said, 'Why do you miss him? He's right down the street …' I said, 'Yes, but he's not HERE.' Then my son said, 'Before I was born and I was with Jesus and the angels … the angels showed me a boy and told me his name (he named my boyfriend).'

I was trying to be nonchalant but was totally intrigued by what he was saying. I said something like, 'Really? What else did they say?'

My son replied, 'They showed me a girl and told me her name is Kim,' (that's me) 'and they showed me another girl and told me her name is … (and he mentioned his sister's name).'

He continued on and on, naming family members. Then finally I had to cut him short because I could see that this might take a while. He didn't offer me any more information other than that the angels had showed him all these people who are in his life now, before he was born.

Freda's son seems to have an even bigger awareness of life.

The Beginning of Time

My son John is 11 and doesn't speak about his spirit contact as much as he used to. However, when he was about seven, I asked if he remembered any past lives and his response was, 'Mommy, you needed me. I have loved you since the beginning of time and we have always been together and we will continue to be together as long as God lets us return to Earth.'

OK, that's very cool, right?

Pre-birth Contact

Another unusual phenomenon is pre-natal communication. Either the child or the parents (or both) have a soul connection before the child is born. They seem to reach out to each other across time and space.

This case is especially intriguing because both parents were independently aware of the contact.

Pre-birth Baby Checks Out Future Mum and Dad

I sensed my daughter's soul enter my body whilst I was waiting on a subway platform about two months before I became pregnant with her. I was so sure that I was pregnant at the time that I didn't want to take the MMR test they wanted me to take at work. When I was about two months pregnant with my son he appeared in a vision as a foetus in front of me. I sensed he wanted to find out more about me. Later that day I discovered he had appeared in exactly the same way to my husband. We worked out the timing and figured out that our future son must have appeared to us both at the same time.

My husband and I were so in tune with our young son (understanding and anticipating his needs) that we didn't realize he was speech-delayed until he was almost three years old. I felt the soul of a third child enter my body as I was driving on the parkway. Since I only wanted two children, I told this soul to find someone else who wanted a baby.

I believe the soul went to my cousin (who was taking precautions not to get pregnant at the time!). That baby saved her marriage, so it was good timing!

Kim believes that her son may have visited her daughter and herself before he was born.

Hello, Family

When Amanda was two and a half I started trying to conceive my second child. It was not announced to the family that we were 'trying' and it took us six months to get pregnant. The first month of trying, Amanda spoke to me in the morning about 'the little white boy' in her bedroom. Then a month and a half later she saw him again. This time it was mid-afternoon and I was in her room putting her down for her nap when she pointed him out to me, but I couldn't see him.

The third and final time she saw him was about three months later. She told me about him in the morning. 'Mommy, the little white boy is gone now.' I asked where he went. She said, 'He went to be with his momma.' That was the last time we'd tried to get pregnant, the evening she's talking about. And we didn't do anything after that. And would you believe, I took a pregnancy test within a couple of weeks and found out that that last attempt 'took'. I told myself, 'I bet I'm pregnant with a boy.' And, sure enough, I was.

But there's more ... one month before I conceived my son, I had been talking to the spirits about allowing me to see any future babies I might be carrying. That night in a dream I clearly saw my future son! And he definitely looked the same when he was born. I was born with black hair which later turned blonde. My husband was born blonde, then turned light brown. My daughter was born with red hair that turned blonde. I had NO idea what colour my son's hair would be! In the dream he showed me a very pale boy dressed in blue, sitting in my daughter's infant car seat. And this pale little boy had dark brown hair and lots of it. That was my son when he was born! The face was the same, too, but that's hard for me to prove since I did not draw a sketch the morning after that dream. Maybe I should've thought of that!

Fascinating stuff! It's such a wide subject that I don't have room to cover more than a few sample stories here … not in this book, anyway. Do you have stories of your own childhood past-life memories? Let me know … maybe we'll write them up in the next book!

CHAPTER 9

Coping with a Psychic Child

The miracle is not to fly in the air or to walk on the
water; but to walk on the Earth.

Chinese proverb

It was hard to decide whether to call this chapter 'Coping with' or the slightly more positive 'Working with' a psychic child. I decided that after looking at all the available information, most people just need to know how to cope!

The suggestions in this chapter are just that: suggestions. Each parent and carer must decide on the best approach for his or her own child. It is my hope that you find ideas here which you may not yet have tried but which may help you to develop your child's abilities or just handle the difficulties of having a psychic child. Maybe you can adapt some of them to help you in your own unique situation.

Parents' Advice

> Having two psychic children of my own, the best advice
> I can offer is to remain open and let the children guide
> you … my kids have guided me and, as a result, my own
> psychic abilities have come forth and I actually enjoy the
> whole thing! – Paula

Indigo Child, Crystal Child, Rainbow Child … the Children of the 'New Earth'

Over the last few years there has been a trickle of books relating to the Indigo, Crystal and Rainbow Children. It's a belief that the new psychic children have come in waves, starting with the 'first batch' who are commonly called the Indigo Children (because of their indigo-coloured auras or biofields).

According to the authors of *The Indigo Children,* Jan Tober and Lee Carroll, the Indigo Child is a boy or girl who displays a new and unusual set of psychological attributes, revealing a pattern of behaviour generally undocumented before. They suggest they are often diagnosed as having ADD/ADHD, which is also common with the stories that have come across my own desk.

The Indigos are the transitional generation, acting as a bridge and making way for the next wave of helpers, the Crystal Children. Common amongst the Crystal Children are their large and expressive eyes. They are gentle children, kind, loving and sensitive. Many of the Crystals have the mind-reading abilities we've discussed throughout this book – not easy for the rest of us who are used to our thoughts being private! This is something we will have to get used to as future generations will communicate more and more using telepathic abilities. This is also why many of the Crystal Children develop speech later in life … they don't need words to communicate!

Next come the Rainbow Children. Following on from the earlier 'scouts', the Rainbow Children have had it a little easier. Their gifts may be a little more scary for their adult carers, as we are no longer able to deny their psychic abilities, which are a natural part of their world. We've already seen some of the developing sixth-sense abilities out there, and there are many more to come. The new kids are here!

The most sceptical of doctors, healthcare workers, religious leaders, teachers and parents are now saying, 'What the heck is going on?' It's not so much sci-fi as real life. It's no longer easy to ignore and, believe it or not, we are the ones who have to adjust!

Sue's son is a Crystal Child … and he told her before she had time to think about it! We've already seen one story about Declan (in Chapter 8), so here's an update.

A Crystal Child

Sometimes when we are driving along in the car, Declan will wake up and say, 'McDonald's,' or 'Sweeties,' then go straight back to sleep at the exact point of passing either a McDonald's or a sweet shop. He doesn't ever remember doing this.

A week or so ago, we had a flurry of snow in the Midlands (we live in Coventry in the UK). Declan had been saying that he had wanted to see snow. We just laughed it off and told him, 'It's not going to snow hard, son.' Declan didn't believe us and just said, 'Well, will you wake me up when the snow is here?' and went to bed. We thought nothing of it until we were getting ready for bed that evening at around 9.30 p.m. and I looked outside (I'm not sure why) and there was about half an inch of snow on the ground. My husband and I laughed and decided we'd better wake our son up as we'd promised. Declan wasn't at all surprised and said, 'I told you the snow was coming!'

I walk on crutches and have only recently got out of a wheelchair. My son cannot remember me before I was taken ill, so has only ever known me in either a wheelchair or on crutches, yet he has persistently said to me, 'Mummy, I can't wait until we run along the beach together.' He keeps telling me this, but if I ask when or where he doesn't know, but is certain it will happen and that 'It will be great fun.' I only hope that it will be soon, as I have been unable to walk properly since 2003!

The most extreme thing that has happened was just as I was looking on your website after reading one of your books. I had read nearly the entire book in just one afternoon, and was struck by the chapter called

'Children's Heavenly Gifts'. I had never heard of terms such as 'Crystal Child' or 'Indigo Child' before, and was enthralled by the 'Born Again' experience.

I finished the book just as my husband brought my two children home from school. There were the usual 'How has school been? What did you have for lunch? Did you have a nice day?' sort of conversations, then we went about our usual after-school habits like making dinner, etc.

Then my son came up to me to ask if I could remove the wrapper from his ice-cream pudding. As I was doing this I jokingly said to him, 'You always get in a mess with these, don't you? You're a pain in the bum, aren't you?' We both laughed and then he said, 'No, Mummy, I'm not a pain in the bum. I'm a Crystal Child … who is a good child.' I looked at him as he happily walked into the kitchen to put his rubbish in the bin, and then I called to my husband and told him what had happened. He was as stunned as I was. I now want to explore this further as Declan had never said this before, ever.

Throughout this book we have explored many types of phenomena, and I have mainly avoided using these specific terms to describe the children … not because I don't believe in the different types – I do – but because sometimes it's hard to see where one type of psychic child leads into the next. There are some fascinating books on the subject if you want to learn more. See the Further Reading and Resources section at the end of the book.

Practical Exercises – Handling Psychic Phenomena in Your Child

Here is another Sue. She sent me this experience relating to her own grandson.

A Friend Called Brian

I haven't thought about Levi being psychic or having a gift, but something we talked about today has set me thinking. Let me explain.

When he was about three he had a friend, lots of parents call them imaginary friends. I didn't, because to Levi this friend was real.

Levi told me his friend's name was Brian. I asked him if he went to school and he replied, 'Don't be, silly, Nan. He's four and goes to nursery.' As Levi was three and Brian was four, this made Brian a year older than Levi. Levi was the only person who could see Brian. My daughter, Levi's mum, never once called Brian his 'imaginary' friend. She simply went along with what he said.

One day they all got back in the car after shopping. Simon (Levi's dad) started to drive, when Levi started more or less shouting and crying at the same time. His dad stopped the car and asked him what was wrong, and Levi said, 'You've left Brian at the bus stop!' They backed up the car, opened the door and let Brian in.

It was nice to know that his mom and dad never mocked him about Brian. Levi sees Brian when he is upset about things, but not if he has been sent to his room for being naughty. He said Brian doesn't come then, only when he was upset.

Levi said Brian comes if he calls him, too. Recently I asked him how old Brian was now and he replied that he must be about ten because he is the same height as him, which makes Brian still a year older than Levi. Levi can't remember all the things they talk about but he did say that the things Brian says make him feel a lot better.

Levi can't tell me what Brian wears because he says he doesn't know, yet he says he can't see through Brian, as he is as solid as we are. He sees him mostly in his bedroom. He knows he is the only one who can see Brian, but this doesn't scare him at all.

Many parents are worried about what to 'do' with invisible friends. Invisible friends can often appear when there are emotional problems within a child's life (new baby, house move, death of a family member, abuse, etc.). The invisible friend can help them to deal with issues or talk about problems which they might not otherwise be able to. This needs to be considered before deciding that an invisible friend is a spirit.

The difficulty is that we often don't know the difference between a 'real' spirit visitor and an imaginary friend. I have asked the many parents who have written to me how they have coped with the phenomenon.

In most cases, acknowledging the invisible friend seems to work best of all. Usually invisible friends (both real and imagined) seem to serve a useful purpose and arise out of a need for comfort or support.

My postbag suggests that requests from your child for intervention are usually simple and include things such as:

- setting an extra place at the table
- holding the door open for the friend
- saying goodnight or goodbye to the friend.

Gentle probing can reveal more information (casually, of course!). Sometimes these friends turn out to be deceased family relatives. Don't panic! These visitors come in love. You might come across one or all of the following:

- Your child chatting away in an empty room. The conversation immediately stops when you appear.
- Your child asking questions and then leaving a gap as if another person is answering.
- Your child appearing to listen to the answer to questions she has asked.
- You may find you receive advice or guidance to questions you have been struggling with in your own life … your child will likely have no idea what your 'message' means, even though it is full of meaning for *you*.
- Your child will recognize his invisible friend in family photographs or old newspaper cuttings, if for example there had been a tragedy in the area (or

the house) in the past. The invisible friend may be known to you or others as a deceased relative.

- You may receive messages from the 'other side' through your child.
- Your child becomes fascinated by a topic which he or she previously had no interest in. A new interest in trains might be as a result of 'chatting' to a deceased great-granddad who was also interested in the subject.
- Your child may give his or her visitor a name.

As long as these visits do not interfere too much in your (or your child's) day-to-day life, do not worry about the experience. If your child is being kept awake at night, you can insist that the visitors visit at a more appropriate time (just as you might make this request of living visitors).

Either a) ask your child to make the request or b) request it yourself (yes, chatting to the 'empty' room may be embarrassing, but it usually works).

Here is one mum's experience.

George

My name is Hannah and my daughter Maddie is a spiritual child. She's so advanced in her speech, and what she comes out with amazes people. She's got a spirit friend whom she calls George. She plays with him at home and at her nan's house; and when she goes to the park, George comes too.

Once when we were at my mum's house and Maddie was in the bath, she turned to me and her nan and told us that George had got out. We asked her who he was and she told us, 'He's a baby.'

Another time at my mum's I was on the computer when Maddie started shouting, 'Hang on a minute, boy ... hang on.' Then she trotted off to the kitchen where I could hear her chatting away to someone. I swear that there was no one there but Maddie and me.

Once she told me that I had a man standing at the end of my bed. When I asked her who it was she said, 'It's a man, Mummy, with a hat on.' I knew who the man was because my dad always used to wear a baseball cap.

I'm always hearing her talking away to someone when there's no one there. She loves animals and being out of doors. That's when she's at her happiest. She also loves fairies, angels, crystals and anything that sparkles.

Invisible friends can be many things, and some children have different types of relationships with many 'unseen' friends, sometimes all at once, like in this next case. A parent's role can be a nightmare and there are no ground rules (or any rules, come to think of it), only suggestions.

Friends?

When my son was two, he developed three imaginary friends: 'Jack' (who is sometimes an old man and sometimes a boy, and very often bad), 'Bum' (who is a little

boy and my son's best friend), and Plato (whom my son
says he made up and isn't really real).

Imaginary friends can be quite normal, but these
three make me wonder – especially Jack, who does bad
things and of whom my son seems frightened sometimes.

Not every spirit visitor is welcome, as Zea knows only
too well:

Good v Bad?

My daughter says she can 'feel' whether the spirits are
good or bad. We have no problem with the 'good' ones,
but the 'bad' ones tend to freak her out.

I think my kids don't like to talk about the more
malevolent ones they see because I think they are worried that just talking about them will get their attention,
and naturally no child wants to spend their day even
thinking about anything negative or scary.

When I was young, my mother (who is also psychic) taught me that prayer is the best way to dispel any
negative energy. I have found that it works for me, so I
have taught my kids to do the same. I have heard that
visualizing white light surrounding them helps. I also tell
my kids that no spirit can hurt you unless you give them
permission to hurt you. Just say, 'No – go away.'

Some people just prefer not to believe certain
things because, let's face it, the unknown can sometimes

be a frightening thing. My dad was exactly the same way … closed-minded and sarcastic about the whole thing.

I picked up a lot of scepticism from my dad, and lost a lot of my own abilities during my adolescence and young adult years. I actually thought my mom was nuts when she spoke of things she saw. When these things started happening to my own kids, I began to remember my abilities as a child and they have started to come back. I have a lot of respect for my mom now.

Mischievous spirits often seem more scary to the parents than the child, as in the following story (although this sounds like a very friendly spirit indeed, and is most likely an older relative who is popping back to visit the new family member from the other side of life).

Bear Cheek!

My grandson saw things at a very early age. His mum told me that one morning she heard him in his cot giggling. He has a very infectious giggle! When she went into his bedroom there was a teddy bear, quite a big one, balanced on the side of the cot! Now, when you think of the size of the side of the cot (about two inches at the most), you can imagine that this freaked her out a little!

Practical Exercises – Troublesome Visitors

From time to time a spirit or 'off-world' (ET) visitor becomes a disruption or a problem. We've already looked at some scenarios in the book and some suggestions for handling difficult visitors; let's go over a few of them again here.

- **Prayer.** You can use the Lord's Prayer, a prayer which relates to your own religion, or even make one up. Prayer is a way of talking to God, so feel free to ask for God (the creator, goddess, the 'supreme being' or your own creator being) to protect you. Prayer can be very powerful indeed, so if you feel comfortable with this, teach your own children how to pray.
- **Just say no**! Teach your children to get in control of what they see. Most 'bad' spirits are just annoying, i.e. they know that your child can see them and they want to communicate or get your child to pass on a message. As your child gets older this might be something they want to do, but as a young child this is a bit of a burden. Teach your child to tell the spirits this (or shout if necessary) … only for the pesky ones, of course!

Useful phrases might include, 'Go away!' or simply 'No!' Practise saying this with your child so he is at ease with using a powerful and commanding voice (in the same way you might get him to practise speaking to any strangers who outstay their welcome!).

- **Learn more.** Talk about the different ways that the spirits appear to your child. As we have already seen, children soon learn to identify passive spirits and those which are out for trouble.
- **Use psychic tools.** Use protection tools such as crystals (for more information see pages 241–2), pictures or figurines of powerful 'protection figures' like angels or crosses (or symbols of protection relating to your family's religious beliefs).
- **Teach your child protection visualizations.**
  - **White-light protection** – ask your child to imagine she is surrounded by a bright white fluffy cloud. Good spirits can come through the cloud; bad spirits cannot.
  - **Mirrors** – ask your child to imagine he is surrounded by mirrors facing outwards. Mirrors bounce back good energy to whoever sends it, and negative energy back from whence it came!
  - **Angel guards** – ask your child to imagine a very large and powerful angel standing behind her. No spirit can come close unless the angel gives permission. Let the child name her angel.

If your child has difficulties with this type of 'imagining', get her to draw a picture to help her create the image in her mind first of all. Never underestimate the power of these types of visualizations!

Tracy has had success with the following method:

Set Some Ground Rules!

I have told my six-year-old that he can only talk to the spirits that are surrounded by good intentions and are friendly.

When he was younger we had a little spirit named Daniel that would make Jake do silly things, and at times bad things. We had a 'talk' with the spirit and my son said Daniel wanted to stay and would try to be better. Jake was three at the time and so was Daniel.

My son has three other spirits that he talks with on a regular basis, and they all seem to keep each other in check and provide a great deal of comfort to my son, so we're happy about it.

Other mums have their own ideas. Jan suggests, 'Get your child to surround themselves with the white light of the Holy Spirit, and do the same with your home. I do this every day as one of our protection tools.'

Dealing with Negative Entities

Emma wrote to tell me about the problems that she and her family were having at home.

My daughter, who is three years old, has an imaginary friend. She speaks about a woman who will hurt Mummy if I go into her bedroom. She also told her dad that there was a man shouting at him, and asked him why he didn't talk to the stranger.

Don't you just want to say, 'Enough already! This is MY house!'? Sometimes it's good to get cross with these spirits. Luckily, in most cases invisible friends are harmless … and, in fact, usually beneficial. If the entity is a friend, then that is fine, but the woman visitor sounds more than a little unhelpful, and spirits should never be allowed to affect your child's life in a negative way. I am unhappy about the fact that the invisible friend says that she will harm the mother here. That is wrong and, in any event, if the woman were a physical being you know you would feel the need to do something about this.

The man shouting at her dad? It's likely to be a relative trying to get his attention.

I told Emma that she was not totally helpless in this situation and there were several things she could try, starting off with a gentle approach. Here were my suggestions:

At bedtime, if your daughter says she can see this woman, you can ask her to leave and tell her she is not welcome. This might be enough in itself.

- If this doesn't work, you can try clearing/cleansing the room. Are there things in the room which belonged to previous owners (curtains or carpets, for example)? These might have belonged to a previous owner who is attracted to them, even from the other side of existence. Often these entities are unaware they are dead and may wonder why you are living in their house. She may see you as a threat in her house. Sometimes just painting the room a fresh new colour or changing the curtains, for example, might be enough to remove the entity.

- You can also employ a cleansing ritual, which can be most beneficial. One example is smudging – you can buy smudge-sticks or smudging wands from the Internet or your local 'New Age' store. These bundles of dried white sage can be used to drive out negative entities. What you need:
  o smudge stick
  o ashtray
  o candle
  o matches or lighter
  o tray
  o large feather (quill size).
- Place all the items together on a tray. Light the candle and use the candle to light the end of the smudge wand. The flame will usually go right out, but if it doesn't, blow it out. Use the smoke and waft it around the room (traditionally a feather would be used for this). Take the smoke into all corners of the room and even waft a little into cupboards and under the bed if you feel it is necessary. Be careful not to damage fabrics or furnishings. Many famous TV psychics use this technique – it works! One wand would easily do a whole house, and may likely be used several times.

- You could also raise the energy of the room by placing fresh flowers (or a flowering plant) in the room – making sure your child is not allergic, of course!

- Another way of lifting the energy of the room is to use pure essential oils in an oil burner. Following the instructions from the manufacturer of your burner, place a couple of drops of oil into the well at the top (in water) and infuse into the room. Try frankincense (I have found this to be very powerful), rose, basil or cedarwood pure essential oils. You only need a couple of drops. If you're using an aromatherapy candle, make sure never to leave a naked flame burning in your child's room. Always supervise! Better yet, infuse your oils into the room whilst you sit in there, and read a book or listen to relaxing music together. An hour should be plenty.

Try following simple Feng Shui techniques of space-clearing. Remove old and broken toys from the room, store and label toys neatly, remove clothes and shoes which your child has outgrown. Wash windows, vacuum the carpet or wash the floor; change the sheets on the bed and open the windows wide to thoroughly air the room. All of these things can have a wonderful effect in changing the energy of a space.

Play 'angel-type' or classical music in the room.

Add a figure of protection – something simple like a pretty picture of an angel or an angel figurine to sit upon a shelf. (This gives permission for higher-energy beings like angels to protect the child and the room.)

At this early stage it is fairly easy to sort out these things yourself. Have a go at one or more of the suggestions above. Stay positive and don't be afraid! You can handle this.

If at any time the problem becomes worse, bring in specialist advice. Your local church may be able to assist, or your nearest New Age store may know people who can help. You may need to bring in a medium who can see or speak to the spirit. If possible, get a personal recommendation and do check if there is a charge (and make sure you know what is involved).

Young Sami had her mum help email the following message: 'I am still learning what all I am able to do. I used to be scared of my gifts but not any more. My mom has helped to teach me not to be scared, just to accept and ask questions if I don't understand.'

I think this shows how important family are when it comes to how well kids cope with their gifts. Our reaction is a good indication as to how stable they are!

More Mums' Suggestions

This mum says that maybe the spirits just need to be acknowledged that they are there and can communicate if we like. She says,

A similar situation happened to me and it seems that as soon as I acknowledged it was happening and would ask them to leave us alone, they did. I do sometimes get glimpses of them, but mainly they are just 'there'. I made it very clear that only positive, godly spirits were welcome.

Our two-year-old will communicate and see a small child and an older man spirit once in a while, and it seems that once I accepted it was happening, they backed down and were peaceful.

Success with Guardian Angels

After several parents (and grandparents) on my Psychic Children Forum had difficulties with spirit visitors I suggested using the guardian angels as 'bouncers'. Several responded, so I thought it might be worth including a couple of their experiences here.

I just wanted to thank Jacky for all her help and advice in regards to my son. He spoke with his guardian angel tonight and we found out his name. We both asked 'Zac', his guardian angel, to protect him and guard him against bad spirits. Your advice has made us feel so much more in control now. I told him that this could be fun, and he liked that idea too …

Here is another one using the same technique:

My son, too, has never slept well and is hysterical when he sees 'glass-like' people, as he describes them. One spirit in particular won't leave his room. My son also describes being able to see spirits in his mind and hear them speak. He is nearly eight and has been quite psychic since the age of 18 months. Tonight we took Jacky's advice and called upon his guardian angel to protect him. He seemed much more at ease as he could see that I looked in control of the situation ...

Sharon called the angels on her daughter's behalf:

My daughter Natalie started getting panic attacks in October 2004 when she was ten. After a couple of months of hell, with very little support from doctors, etc., I contacted a psychic who connected with angels. She said Natalie was very worried about starting a new school in September 2005, and gave me some prayers to say for her to the Archangels Michael and Raphael. I was delighted when she improved almost immediately and became a much stronger and more confident child during 2005, and after starting her new school absolutely loved it.

Annette had some great ideas, too, so I have edited them from her posting:

My daughter started seeing spirits everywhere this past summer, and life has never been the same for us. I've been seeking out people to help us with what she is seeing and experiencing as well. This is what we have learned:

1. Suggest to your children or grandchildren that they pray before going to bed, remembering to post guardian angels at each corner of the bed.

2. Get them to imagine a protective bubble of white light around them and their bed all night long.

3. Suggest they use their 'imagination' [what we call 'imagination' is a powerful force of creation in other realms] and see all other spirits fade away as the angels protect them whilst they sleep. (Angels are our guardian spirits, but respect our free will and do not come unless we call upon them and request what we need.)

4. Ask your children if they have a spirit guide. Ask if that guide has a name. Your child can call on his spirit guide as well to keep the annoying spirits away.

5. Let your children know that spirits are around us all the time and that there are more and more children who are being born who can see them, too.

6. Some of the spirits they will see are: their own guides and angels; people they have had past lives with who pop in to visit (depending on your view of reincarnation, you may or may not want to bring this up); spirits who are just passing through; spirits who have had a connection to the house they live in or on the land; spirits who are drawn to them because they understand that they can be seen by

the child and who may want to try and contact others who are still living.

7. Someone recommended to me that I watch *Ghost Whisperer* on TV. I haven't seen it yet, but it is about a woman who has seen spirits since childhood.

I love this series. The CBS show is also shown in the UK and stars Jennifer Love Hewitt as Melinda Gordon, a medium who communicates with earthbound spirits (ghosts) who still have problems with the living. But back over to Annette:

I know with my daughter, her spirit vision has a definite time-frame. She usually starts seeing them around four in the afternoon, and they get more numerous and easier to see as the evening progresses. This can make walking alone through a dark room or going to bed a difficult experience for her. Even getting out of the car and walking to the front door causes her anxiety as she sees all kinds of things around her.

I keep explaining to her that they are all around even during the daytime, but the daylight makes them harder to see. They are just hanging out and won't harm her. She did have a few experiences where she was touched. I was told by a psychic that the spirits are trying to get her attention and want to communicate because they know she can see them.

I am lucky enough to live in an area where there are Mind, Body and Spirit fairs [alternative healing and psychic-type events] every few months. I doubted my daughter at first and then went for a reading at one of these fairs and several psychics came over to me, looked me in the eye and said, 'Do you know what you have here in your daughter?' I sat with several of them for 15-minute sessions and just listened, wrote down what they said and tried to reach some kind of cohesive understanding of it all. They knew she had these special talents.

As a woman, when I was pregnant I went to all the prenatal classes, exercise classes and read all I could. I understood what to expect in terms of physical and mental development. Nobody ever offered me a class in having a psychic child. Psychic Infant 101 was not a course given in college. We just have to learn as we go along on this one.

You're right, Annette! After many years of working with the parents and grandparents of psychic children, I realized the same thing. It seems we all learn as we go along, so it makes sense to share everything we have discovered. Often it really is just trial and error. Of course, it's always easier if we can learn from others!

I wanted to just share this final story about our children's visitors. Emma has no idea who her daughter's invisible friends are … but apparently there are a lot of them.

Kiddies

My daughter Maryellen is six years old. Since she was two, Maryellen has talked about her 'kiddies'. She has always been consistent in saying that there are lots and lots of them and that they are always with her.

When small she would cry if we didn't keep the door open so her kiddies could get in (this could take a while). One time Maryellen had hysterics at a train station because one of her kiddies was on the track and was going to get run over. Another time we were out shopping when she told us that one of her kiddies' eyes had fallen out and she was going to buy some new ones!

As Maryellen is getting older she mentions her kiddies less, but they do still come up, especially one she calls 'crying kid,' as he cries all the time.

Practical Exercises – Training Up Your Young Healer

The imagination is a strong force. What we create/think in our minds really does manifest in reality (basic quantum physics) and we all have the ability to heal (to a certain extent) naturally.

When you were a child and you fell over, your mother naturally held you close or 'kissed' your bruises better (hopefully). We comfort people with a hand on their back, or by holding their hand. Healing is as natural as breathing. Comforting relaxes the patient, which in turn releases the body's natural painkiller – endorphins.

The trick is to *not* take on the sickness, and to *not* give away your own personal bodily energy. If you or your child wants to practise healing each other (or you want to try out the technique on your pets), you might enjoy the following.

Remember that healing should never replace the advice and care of your doctor (or vet) but be used in addition or as 'complementary' healing. These techniques can also be used in emergencies and whilst awaiting other treatments.

Your children might also enjoy working on their toys!

- Make sure your 'patient' is relaxed, comfortable and not too chilly.
- Imagine you are both surrounded by God's healing light (think of a white fluffy cloud and you can't go far wrong), or suggest your child imagine their 'patient' surrounded by 'angel light,' which they may see as another colour.
- Ask your guardian angel to help as always (or the Archangel Raphael – the healing angel). Make up some special words or say something along the lines of, 'Guardian angel, I/we welcome your assistance with healing … [add name here], so long as it be in the best interests of … [name] … or with God's will.'

- Sometimes it is a person's 'time', and the best interests of the sick might be to pass gently to the afterlife. Don't take on the responsibility of the healing. The healing is not about you; you are acting as a 'channel' for the healing light.
- Now imagine that this healing light is pouring in through the top of your head and out of your hands. Use this healing light on each other rather than your own energy (remember not to be a 'psychic vampire', taking energy from someone else – nor let anyone 'vampire' you by taking *your* energy).
- Hold your hands over each other, letting the energy flow from your hands until you feel it is time to stop (or your pet walks away!).
- Remember to thank your universal creator (God, the source/god/goddess, etc., according to your spiritual or religious beliefs) afterwards.

In urgent situations you can use this method on yourself, too. I remember being stuck on a train once and it was late at night. I had raging toothache and no painkillers – the self-healing took away the pain and it was brilliant.

In the case of that annoying friend on the phone, 'imagine' the same situation. Ask your own guardian angel to protect you from your friends' 'energy vampiring' and for your friends' guardian angels to receive healing from the 'source' rather than suck you dry (you know when this has happened because you will feel exhausted after giving a listening ear).

Children can easily learn this technique. Another trick is to imagine your friend and their troubles inside a big circle. Don't jump in the circle with them! Hopefully when they are ready they can step out of the circle, leaving their pain behind them. Of course, you can hold out your (spiritual) hand to help!

Using Crystals

Many children like to use crystals in healing, as my own daughter naturally did when she was younger. Children with natural psychic abilities are attracted to crystals even more so. It's as if on some higher level of consciousness they are aware of the healing and magical properties of these beautiful natural stones.

The most suitable crystals for children are tumbled crystals (where the natural, sharp edges are softened and polished by placing the crystals into a professional tumbling machine). These tumbled crystals come in a very wide range of natural colours and varieties, and you can buy them from crystal and New Age stores, gift shops and the Internet. I have even seen them sold from bubble-gum-type dispensing machines at tourist attractions and even bookshops.

A good book on crystals would be a worthwhile purchase if your child has an interest. Although your crystal book will give you the 'traditional' use for each crystal, your children may have other ideas. Let them pick their own crystals for display, healing and comfort.

Be sure to keep the smaller stones away from young children, as they can be a choking hazard. Crystals can be any size, but select for safety and appropriate age of your child.

Collecting Crystals

Crystal collecting can become a fascinating hobby. These pretty stones can be arranged on open shelves (not if you have cats, though, as they tend to roll them all around the house! Try Blu Tack.) or gathered in bowls (some crystal healers believe that each crystal should have its own space, but I like to see all the colours jumbled together). As always in this book I suggest that you and your child empower yourselves and decide on how crystals are going to work in your lives, and what is right for you.

Plastic hobby boxes with individual compartments can be a fun way of sorting and labelling your collection. Here are a few crystals to start your child's collection:

- **clear quartz** – healing stone, increases psychic abilities, offers protection
- **rose quartz** – signifies 'unconditional love'; a beautiful natural energy
- **amethyst** – this purple crystal is also used for psychic protection
- **tiger's eye** – this brown stripy crystal is said to calm teenagers!

- **green jade** – brings calm and serenity
- **citrine** – this yellow quartz is said to bring self-confidence
- **hematite** – shiny black crystal which many believe brings balance
- **jasper** – red jasper is thought of as a crystal with protection properties.

Cleansing Crystals

Many believe that crystals should be regularly cleansed of negative energies which are collected and held within the crystal. Your crystal book will give you plenty of ideas.

If you want to cleanse your crystals together you could draw them (pull them) through the smoke of an incense stick, or hold them in a cool mountain stream. If you don't have a mountain stream handy – and most of us don't – your child could rinse the crystals in a small cup of mineral water and leave them to dry naturally on the windowsill.

Charging Crystals

To 'charge' your crystals, you could place them on a tray and stand them out in the sunlight or moonlight (make sure they are in a safe place and won't get taken or damaged). This certainly adds to the magical feel of your child's crystals, as well as being lots of fun!

Crystals can be charged with different energies and 'asked' to perform different tasks. This is a simple procedure and one your child will enjoy doing. In each case your child holds the crystal after it has been cleaned/ cleansed and 'imagines' and 'asks' the crystal to carry out the task required. It is then ready for use.

If at any time your child wants to change the use of a crystal, cleanse it and charge it again. Don't worry if the ritual is not performed perfectly. Our 'intent' (or the child's intent) is the most important thing here.

Here are some examples:

1. **Sending love to your pet:** Select a rose quartz (or any crystal your child feels is appropriate). Ask the child to hold the rose quartz in her hand and imagine the crystal holding her love and sending it to the pet. Place the charged crystal next to a photograph of the pet (or, for security of the crystal, you can also tape the crystal to the front or back of the frame). Be careful not to place small crystals by the pet, who might consider them food!

2. **Night-time protection crystal:** Select a crystal which is traditionally used for protection, like a clear quartz, or the child can select any crystal which he feels is appropriate. Ask the child to hold the crystal and ask the crystal to protect and look after him. Place the crystal under a pillow in a drawstring bag

or stand it next to the figurine of an angel (or tape it to the angel figurine).

3. **Help with homework:** Select a citrine crystal (or any crystal that your child feels is appropriate). As above, your child holds the crystal and fixes her intent on her desire for the crystal to perform the task requested. Place the citrine on the desk next to where your child works.

Crystals for Healing and Comfort

Children can be very aware of the magical abilities of crystals, and you can make full use of this. Crystals can be used for many things including:

- Difficult new situations (new school, trip away from parents)? – Stitch a crystal into the lining of a coat – or inside the 'heart' of a soft toy.
- Doctor, hospital or dentist visit? – Place a crystal into your child's pocket or, if appropriate, your child could wear a crystal pendant.

A Mum's Experience

I had the idea to let my son pick out some crystals after he was having trouble sleeping (I have a whole bunch). He picked out my big amethyst, a glendonite and one other I can't remember. He had the idea himself to put the amethyst beside the bed, one under his pillow, and he held the glendonite in his hand. He said that it really helped him at night and he hasn't been scared since.

Another mum's suggestion:

Take your child to a stone/crystal store. They are often fond of children in these places. You can work together to make a necklace, or just let her pick out a stone to help her keep her energy field strong and be able to either help the spirits she is afraid of or not attract them at all.

More Ideas

This suggestion came via mum Sherri, who has a wealth of experience in this area:

One coping strategy that my seven-year-old daughter came up with, when people made fun of her seeing angels, was to explain it this way … 'Do you believe in God? Well, you can't see him but you know he's there. It's like that with my angels. I can't show them to you but I can tell you what they do and you can see what they do.'

Mary has another suggestion, one which I can see would be brilliant at calming and relaxing your psychic child.

My daughter Stella is three. My mother-in-law gave her a machine called 'Sound Therapy' (by Conair). It has a selection of different natural sounds on it. They are: tropical forest, thunderstorm, summer night, ocean waves, 'white noise', heartbeat, songbirds, waterfall, running stream and rainfall. Stella loves the songbirds the best and it really helps her to relax.

Keeping a Record of Your Child's Psychic Abilities

In time we learn to deal with pretty much anything. One of the sad things is that we often forget the psychic experiences of childhood. One way to help us remember is to make a record of them in a special notebook, or get your children to make their own records.

This suggestion came from my Psychic Children Forum.

Visual Records

I think that keeping some sort of record is a good idea. When my daughter sees things, I have her draw a picture of it and then date it. I wish I had thought of doing this with my boys when they were younger. Now that they're older (teenagers) they keep a lot of things to themselves.

Kids' Ideas

Kids can often come up with their own solutions, so do ask them what they think. Tracy's son had a unique idea for having a rest from his spirit playmates, nice as they were!

Holiday, Anyone?

We do try to treat the psychic phenomenon normally, as much as possible at least. At times my son will come up with some very interesting facts and it is hard to not be amazed by it all.

I have told him that most people can't see spirits and that he is very lucky to have the ability to see them. Just the other day he told me that sometimes he doesn't want to play with his angels and that he sends them to Disneyland to play for a while, so he can have a break. They can fly anywhere they want, he told me.

I think this gives him a break from all of the surreal aspects of his life and lets him focus on being a five-year-old.

Always ask your children if you are stumped for ways of helping them. You might be amazed at what they come up with.

Problems from Living Souls

Many of the issues in this book have been about parents and grandparents coping with a psychic child, but Sherri made a good point which I wanted to share with you.

> I try not to push my daughter or ask too many ques-
> tions unless she offers information. I don't want her to
> become 'a circus act' with people bombarding her with
> questions. The stress it would be for her to interpret the
> signs correctly at such a young age would be fierce. So
> many people have experienced her gifts that I some-
> times feel the need to protect her from the pressure.

Of course, she's right!

Living with a Psychic Child

Not everyone who reads this book will be psychic or
have psychic children. Some of you will just be curious
about it all, and I hope this has given you a little more
background and something to think about.

Intriguing, fascinating and maybe even frightening,
psychic abilities and paranormal phenomena *are* growing in children. It really is hard to deny that 'something'
at least is going on!

Whether you believe that it's all coincidence, that the
human race is undergoing a normal evolutional change,
or that highly advanced beings from other realms are
incarnating into young human bodies to assist our plan-
etary growth, we certainly need to pay attention to it.

If you have questions or experiences of your own,
then I would love to hear from you. I believe there is so
much more information to come on the subject, and

already I am researching a follow-up book. Maybe you'll be a part of it? One thing's for certain … the future is fascinating!

Further Reading and Resources

My Own and Readers' Recommended Children's Websites, Books and CDs

www.JackyNewcomb.com – My own website, which contains information about psychic children and includes a link to my own forum for psychic children discussion (see also **Forums** below).

www.childspirit.org – a non-profit educational and research organization dedicated to understanding and nurturing the inner life of children and adults.

Forums

groups.yahoo.com/group/psychic_children/ – My own forum dedicated to parents and relatives of psychic children. Free to join.

Books about Children

Carol Bowman, *Children's Past Lives* (Thorsons)
------, *Return from Heaven: Beloved Relatives Reincarnated Within Your Family* (Thorsons)
Cassandra Eason, *Psychic Power of Children* (Foulsham/Quantum)
Trutz Hardo, *Children Who Have Lived Before* (Rider)

Books and Websites about the New Children

Lee Carroll and Jan Tober, *Indigo Celebration* (Hay House)
------, *The Indigo Children: The New Kids Have Arrived* (Hay House)
Lynne Gallagher, *Psychic Kids* (The Mercier Press)
Doreen Virtue, *The Care and Feeding of Indigo Children* (Hay House)
------, *The Crystal Children* (Hay House)
------, *Indigo, Crystal and Rainbow Children* [audio book] (Hay House)
www.akiane.com – site about Akiane Kramarik, the extraordinary child artist

Soul Travel

Dolores Cannon, *Between Death and Life* (Ozark Mountain Publishing Inc)

Dr Michael Newton, *Destiny of Souls* (Llewellyn Worldwide)

------, *Journey of Souls* (Llewellyn Worldwide)

UFOs/Alien/Off-World Visitors

Bonnie Jean Hamilton's website where you can contact her about her experiences:
www.alienabductionhelp.com
Mike Oram – author of *Does It Rain in Other Dimensions? – A True Story of Alien Encounters* (O Books) – www.inotherdimensions.com
Nick Pope www.nickpope.net
Stefan www.paranormalawakening.com
Gary Zukav, *Soul Stories* (Simon and Schuster)

Other Books by the Author

If you have enjoyed this book you may enjoy other books by Jacky Newcomb:

An Angel Treasury (Harper Element)
A Little Angel Love (Harper Element)
An Angel Saved My Side (Harper Element)
An Angel by My Side (Harper Element)
An Angel Held My Hand (Harper Element)
Jacky Newcomb and Alice Geddes-Ward, *A Faerie Treasury* (Hay House)
------, *Angels Watching Over Me* (Hay House)

Notes

Notes

We hope you enjoyed this Hay House book.
If you would like to receive a free catalogue featuring additional
Hay House books and products, or if you would like information
about the Hay Foundation, please contact:

Hay House UK Ltd
292B Kensal Rd • London W10 5BE
Tel: (44) 20 8962 1230; Fax: (44) 20 8962 1239
www.hayhouse.co.uk

***

Published and distributed in the United States of America by:
Hay House, Inc. • PO Box 5100 • Carlsbad, CA 92018-5100
Tel.: (1) 760 431 7695 or (1) 800 654 5126;
Fax: (1) 760 431 6948 or (1) 800 650 5115
www.hayhouse.com

Published and distributed in Australia by:
Hay House Australia Ltd • 18/36 Ralph St • Alexandria NSW 2015
Tel.: (61) 2 9669 4299; Fax: (61) 2 9669 4144
www.hayhouse.com.au

Published and distributed in the Republic of South Africa by:
Hay House SA (Pty) Ltd • PO Box 990 • Witkoppen 2068
Tel./Fax: (27) 11 467 8904 • www.hayhouse.co.za

Published and distributed in India by:
Hay House Publishers India • Muskaan Complex • Plot No.3
B-2 • Vasant Kunj • New Delhi – 110 070.
Tel.: (91) 11 41761620; Fax: (91) 11 41761630.
www.hayhouse.co.in

Distributed in Canada by:
Raincoast • 9050 Shaughnessy St • Vancouver, BC V6P 6E5
Tel.: (1) 604 323 7100; Fax: (1) 604 323 2600

***

Sign up via the Hay House UK website to receive the Hay House
online newsletter and stay informed about what's going on with
your favourite authors. You'll receive bimonthly announcements
about discounts and offers, special events, product highlights,
free excerpts, giveaways, and more!
www.hayhouse.co.uk